PLANNING, MONITORING
AND EVALUATION IN DEVELOPMENT
ORGANISATIONS

Despite the many manuals and toolkits available, PME continues to pose difficulties to project planners and managers. In this volume, De Coninck et al. offer a user-focused, practice-grounded way to approach PME training and facilitation in civil society organisations. Useful suggestions, like adopting a 'total organisation' approach to PME—thus reconciling PME and organisational learning, and many examples taken from the authors' extensive field experience—make this volume provocative and supportive reading for PME practitioners.

Teobaldo Pinzas, Director, ETC-Andes, Peru

This is one of the most accessible documents currently available for improving PME skills and systems of organizations working in the field of international development. This book will be useful for anyone working within NGOs as well as for facilitators of (short) training courses on results-based management.

Kees Biekart, Senior Lecturer, Institute of Social Studies (ISS),
The Hague, The Netherlands

Amazing document, especially considering the clever presentation of practical and conceptual material nicely intertwined with captivating light touches.

Tom Olila, Consultant in Organisation Capacity Building
and Finance Management, Kenya

An inspiring book for development practitioners, facilitators, trainers and consultants. A comprehensive source of inspiration and information for everyone involved in developing and improving PME in organisations. The book provides an open-minded and thorough reflection about PME concepts from an organisational perspective. It offers a wide range of practical experiences that are presented in a clear-cut, concrete and applicable manner. Essential reading for development professionals, a book to use and refer to over and over!

Jan Kuyper, Management for Development Foundation,
Training & Consultancy, The Netherlands

This book has synthesised the real PME experiences of NGOs across continents. It captures a wide perspective of PME, with a 'total organization approach', instead of a fragmented and reductionist approach of a single programme or activity. It strongly advocates and assists NGOs to customise their PME system as it considers each NGO as unique in its context. The book lays strong emphasis on learning and a process approach for PME. To learn, prove, and improve, it encourages formal, informal and participatory PME approaches. The constant learning process thus becomes a central theme of PME. Every NGO and all their stakeholders would immensely benefit from this book to enhance effectiveness, sustainability and a sense of programme ownership by the stakeholders.

Malla Reddy, Director, Accion Fraterna, India

This book is a valued addition to the available resources in the PME world, an interesting text for PME facilitators and those who are concerned with result-oriented planning, monitoring and evaluation of development interventions, whether at programme or organisational level. It offers a good combination of process-focused field examples and conceptual frameworks, without loading the concepts with theories on planning, monitoring or evaluation. The practical tips bring the readers to real life situations, as the analysis is supported by examples from various contexts across Asia, Africa and Europe. The book can be used both as a training guide and a handbook on planning PME for proving and improving.

M. Ehsanur Rahman, Deputy Director,
Dhaka Ahsania Mission, Bangladesh

PLANNING, MONITORING AND EVALUATION IN DEVELOPMENT ORGANISATIONS

SHARING TRAINING AND FACILITATION EXPERIENCES

JOHN DE CONINCK, KHILESH CHATURVEDI,
BEN HAAGSMA, HANS GRIFFIOEN
AND MARIECKE VAN DER GLAS

Los Angeles • London • New Delhi • Singapore
www.sagepublications.com

First published in 2008 by

SAGE Publications India Pvt Ltd
B1/I-1 Mohan Cooperative Industrial Area
Mathura Road, New Delhi 110 044, India
www.sagepub.in

SAGE Publications Inc
2455 Teller Road
Thousand Oaks, California 91320, USA

SAGE Publications Ltd
1 Oliver's Yard, 55 City Road
London EC1Y 1SP, United Kingdom

SAGE Publications Asia-Pacific Pte Ltd
33 Pekin Street
#02-01 Far East Square, Singapore 048763

Second Printing 2009

Published by Vivek Mehra for SAGE Publications India Pvt Ltd, typeset in 11/13 pt Minion, printed at Chaman Enterprises, New Delhi.

Library of Congress Cataloging-in-Publication Data

Planning, monitoring and evaluation in development organisations: sharing training and facilitation experiences/by John De Coninck (et al.).

    p. cm.

Includes bibliographical references.

    1. Economic development projects—Management.   2. Economic assistance. 3. Non-governmental organisations—Management.   4 Non-profit organisations—Management.   I. De Coninck, John.

    HD75.8.P625   338.91068'3—dc22   2008   2008014315

ISBN: 978-81-7829-857-3 (Pb)

The SAGE Team: Sugata Ghosh, Abantika Banerjee, Amrita Saha and
Trinankur Banerjee

CONTENTS

CONTENTS

LIST OF BOXES

LIST OF ABBREVIATIONS

ACDEP	Association of Church Development Projects
AF	Accion Fraterna
ASK	Association for Stimulating Know-how
CBO	community-based organisation
CDRN	Community Development Resource Network
CORDAID	Catholic Organisation for Relief and Development Aid
CSC	Centre de Services aux Coopératives
DANIDA	Danish International Development Agency
DELTA-C	Centre de Formation et d'Appui Conseil pour le Développement Local
ECAD	Education et Coordination pour l'Agriculture Durable
EU	European Union
EWS	early warning system
GTZ	Deutsche Gesellschaft für Technische Zusammenarbeit
IC	ICCO/CORDAID Consult
ICCO	Inter-church Organisation for Development Cooperation
ICSK	International Christelijk Steurfonds Kenia (International Christian Support Fund in Kenya)
IIRR	International Institute for Rural Reconstruction
ILS	internal learning system
LFA	logical framework analysis
MDGs	millennium development goals
M&E	monitoring and evaluation
NGO	non-governmental organisation
OD	organisation development
OOPP	objective-oriented participatory planning
PBME	planning, budgeting, monitoring and evaluation
PGCS	Purvanchal Gramin Chetna Samiti
PME	planning, monitoring and evaluation
POCC	Pool for Organizational Change and Capacity
PRA	participatory rural appraisal
PREFED	Programme Régional de Formation et d'Echanges pour le Développement
PRSPs	poverty reduction strategy papers
RPL	Réseau Plaidoyer et Lobby
SMART	specific, measurable, achievable, relevant, time-bound

TRICOM	Tri-People Consortium for Peace, Progress and Development of Mindanao
TAABCO	Transforming, Analysing, Accompanying and Building Change Organisations
TEDDO	Teso Diocese Planning and Development Office
USAID	United States Agency for International Development
WUAs	water users' associations
ZOPP	ziel orientierte projektplanung

PREFACE

Over the last few years, a group of 20 trainers and facilitators from Africa, Asia and Europe met on several occasions to share experiences, specifically on supporting development organisations to enhance their planning, monitoring and evaluation (PME) practice. These meetings elicited a rich variety of examples, success stories and challenges.

Such variety signals the increasingly rigorous demands placed upon development agencies, including civil society organisations, to design and use well-structured monitoring and evaluation systems, and to link these to their planning cycles. It also mirrors a growing realisation that sustainable development is premised upon the existence of vibrant learning organisations with effective PME systems.

The meetings provided an opportunity to reflect on the challenges that arise from this growing need for sound PME practice. Indeed, at the mention of monitoring and evaluation, or PME, many have a tendency to see donor conditionality or, quite simply, to run away. Yet, is any daily action, since birth, not informed by what professionals like to call a PME cycle of one type or another? Are we not constantly surrounded by PME in many guises and disguises? In spite of this, it seems that practice has become increasingly technocratic, intellectualised and monopolised by often inflexible PME specialists, instead of enhancing the learning capabilities that are essential for organisational survival and for sustainable development: PME for improving, as well as PME for proving.

As a group of PME facilitators and trainers, we therefore asked ourselves, 'Can we share our real-life experiences, our successes and our suggestions to tackle PME facilitation challenges?' As we reflected on this, we started to develop the elements of a PME approach that is context- and organisation-specific, and in tune with local culture. In other words, a 'total organisation approach' going beyond projects, or programmes, to include important contextual influences originating from both within and outside the organisation, as well as the often neglected financial dimension of organisational life.

This volume presents the fruit of our reflection. It is based on notes and examples from our respective practices in the South and is meant for use by PME facilitators and practitioners, whether they are working in non-governmental organisations (NGOs), in other development organisations, or as desk officers in donor agencies.

We gratefully acknowledge the contributions to our discussions over the years of Nereah Makau from Transforming, Analysing, Accompanying and Building Change Organisations (TAABCO), Isaac Bekalo and John Adede from the International Institute for Rural Reconstruction (IIRR), all in Kenya; of Malex Alebikiya from the Association of Church Development Projects (ACDEP) in Ghana; of Janvière Mukantwali, from the Programme Régional de Formation et d'Echanges pour le Développement (PREFED) in Rwanda; of Lúcia Helsloot, Peter de Keijzer and Wim Spierings from the Catholic Organisation for Relief and Development Aid (CORDAID) in the Netherlands; of Mamadou Keita, from the Centre de Formation et d'Appui Conseil pour le Développement Local (DELTA-C) in Mali; and of Ambrose Ongwen from ICCO/ CORDAID Consult (IC Consult).

We especially thank Corinne Canlas from Pool for Organizational Change and Capacity (POCC) in the Philippines, Betsy Mboizi and Edwin Kayuki from the Community Development Resource Network (CDRN) in Uganda, Ehsanur Rahman from the Dhaka Ahsania Mission in Bangladesh, and Anirban Ghose from Pradan in India, who contributed to our text. Thanks also go to our illustrator, Mr Ras, from Uganda. Finally, we are grateful to our four reviewers who commented on an earlier draft of this book: Rick Davies, Irene Guijt, Emma Rotondo and Jim Woodhill.

Any shortcomings are, however, the responsibility of our core group of co-authors: Khilesh Chaturvedi (from the Association for Stimulating Know-how [ASK] in India), Ben Haagsma (IC Consult, the Netherlands), Mariecke van der Glas (ICCO, Nicaragua), Hans Griffioen (IC Consult) and John De Coninck (independent consultant in Uganda), who also edited this volume.

We are also very grateful to CORDAID and ICCO in the Netherlands: their generous contribution made this publication possible.

PART 1
PME: WHY ARE WE HERE?

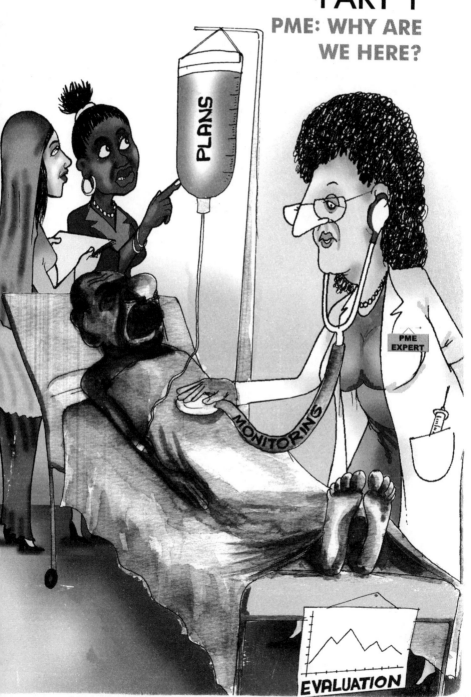

1

OH NO!
NOT ANOTHER PME MANUAL?

WHERE ARE WE COMING FROM?

Planning, monitoring and evaluation (PME) remains a challenge for many development organisations in spite of countless PME workshops, experts and manuals. Yet, we believe that effective PME is essential for organisational survival (and therefore for sustainable development) and that this can be nurtured through careful and sensitive PME training and facilitation. We do not propose here a PME manual: our aim in these pages is rather to share some of our real-life experiences as PME facilitators and to offer suggestions to support PME processes, with a focus on civil society organisations.

As a group of facilitators who have worked on PME issues in different contexts, we realised that we confronted three common challenges:

1. First, a perception of PME as *imposed, 'technical' and expensive.* Partner organisations (those defined here as development organisations that receive, or potentially receive, support from a PME facilitator) often perceive PME as a donor's concern, rather than a way to strengthen learning and to focus on the question, 'What are we here for?' Negative connotations are reinforced when project cycles are rigidly applied, with an emphasis on efficiency and control, with little sensitivity for the informal, the unexpected, or the unplanned. PME work then follows a 'blueprint' approach, neglecting the specificities of organisations, their size, age, culture and type of interventions. We then see a technocratic attitude, with an emphasis on the inflexible application of instruments, often accompanied by a tendency for PME overkill and large expenditure. It also fosters a focus on 'PME for proving', at the expense of 'PME for improving'.

2. Second, in terms of PME *contents,* there is a frequent focus on a particular project, or programme, rather than on the wider organisation, its reason for existence and the broader context in which it operates. Our experiences, for instance, tell us that the cultural context is all-important in PME work, at both the organisational and the broader national levels. Yet, we often fail to take these into account. Furthermore, 'financial PME' is rarely an integral part of this picture, but rather artificially marginalised and left in the sole hands of the 'finance people'.

3. Third, we see PME *support processes* that emphasise training workshops which, however well delivered, seldom lead to successful PME application, let alone sustained use. This reflects the limits of a one-shot method, as opposed to a more process-oriented approach, where PME is about day-to-day activities and attitudes, rather than 'PME events'.

PME: REFLECTION FROM OUR PRACTICE

So why this book? While we work in various countries, for different organisations and in different roles, we propose to share experiences that reflect these common challenges and help to:

1. **Embrace a 'total organisation' approach to PME,** not only rooted in programmes, or projects, but with a wider perspective: that of the 'total organisation', with its financial dimension, its

environment, its collaborators and competitors, in a context informed by local and national cultures. The practice of PME is even influenced by the evolution of a body of ideas about PME itself (see Box 1.1). All these forces are, in our experience, so powerful that any PME process must take them into account to have a chance of sustained use. Building PME skills at the project level might be a good entry point, but we believe that organisational PME processes should be the goal, as only organisation-wide learning will secure organisational survival and, in turn, nurture sustainable development processes.

2. **Enhance custom-made PME.** We have found that PME support is rarely effective if it is not customised to a particular organisation and its stakeholders. This may be a small community-based group, a network with a challenging diversity of interests and needs, or a well-established organisation with an entrenched culture. Each has its own history, values and skills, and faces different challenges in its context, with its multitude of stakeholders. Most often, these have legitimate claims to information and decision-making which, while varied, must all be recognised.

3. **Bring PME into daily learning practice** so that it becomes part of mental processes within a partner organisation, changing mindsets and attitudes, while reflecting contexts and capacities. We have found that PME can be disempowering when the facilitator adopts an 'expert' terminology and method, or when PME fosters a directive, top–down vision of development. We focus here on PME approaches and tools that are participatory and empowering and that move away from the notion that 'there is only one way of doing things'. This does not imply, however, that participation should undermine responsibility for decision-taking: the responsibilities of different people in an organisation, within and amongst different stakeholders, need to be clearly defined for a system to function well.

Empowerment and learning are linked and we thus emphasise 'PME for improving', as well as 'PME for proving'. This can take several forms: respecting and encouraging informal learning, closing the gap between the 'P' of PME and M&E, and linking learning to accountability. It is also related to an understanding of change as often uncertain rather than linear and predictable, and to the characteristics of the organisation itself. These all play an important role in shaping the needs, interest and complexities of PME processes and therefore need to be considered when helping

Box 1.1 PME is Changing...

There was a time when the good intentions of development organisations remained largely unquestioned. No longer: in part because of their growing dependence on institutional donors, hard questions about the quality and relevance of their work are now frequently asked. PME reflects this evolution.

The early emphasis (before the 1990s) of PME was on a 'project approach'. It was then essentially a tool to report—especially to donors—on project work against funds provided. With regard to planning, the early emphasis on participatory planning methods (such as with participatory rural appraisal [PRA] and its derivatives) was complemented by other tools and approaches (project cycle management, objective-oriented participatory planning [OOPP], or ziel orientierte projektplanung [ZOPP] and logical framework analysis [LFA]).

Later, PME increasingly reflected a preoccupation with measurable results and demonstrating impact, in addition to financial accountability, often requiring complicated monitoring and evaluation (M&E) systems and practices. This 'impact approach' to PME, reacting against a 'vague', 'ideologically-motivated' perception of development, has not met with universal enthusiasm. It has, for instance, been castigated for being mechanistic, with an overemphasis on improved efficiency, outputs and indicators and over-structured and formalised systems, thus often neglecting qualitative change and informal processes. Lack of good communication between donor agencies and development organisations has thus often persisted and doubts about the quality and focus of investments continue. It is also becoming clear that the complexity of change and the time necessary to achieve any real transformation is often underestimated.

More recently, PME has also focused on 'process and relationships' reflecting a realisation that context is all-important and that more attention is needed to make all 'stakeholders' in (and around) a development organisation accountable for contributing to its effectiveness. This requires some distance from the daily 'doing', more emphasis on why complex changes happen or not, in other words, learning from the emerging so that the very relationships and processes needed to achieve the overall developmental goals are effective.

Much of this evolution can be attributed to the type of field experiences shared in this book. In part, this has shown that PME facilitation, or capacity-building for PME, is more multifaceted than anticipated, a complexity and diversity that should not be taken too lightly, as the following pages illustrate.

to enhance PME practice. We must also cut across artificial (and often harmful) barriers between financial and 'activity PME' and ensure that financial M&E contributes to an organisation's overall planning and to evaluating its performance.

4. **Adopting a process approach to PME support work**, which is more effective, in our experience, than one-off training events and workshops. Developing new approaches and turning them into regular practice involves more than technical fixes–working on organisational culture may, for instance, be necessary. This is a long-term endeavour. A flexible, iterative approach–learning as one goes along–is often required, with a shift in PME support from training to *joint learning*, with constant adjustments, collaborative reviews and re-planning to remain on track. This demands a mix of facilitation approaches to suit particular learning needs at different times and in different circumstances, such as mentoring and coaching, distance learning methods, exchange visits to other organisations facing similar challenges, secondments and internships, in addition to traditional workshops.

Above all, the PME facilitator must be a keen learner, able to adapt method and contents and to shed the clothes of the all-knowing expert, ready to fix PME in an instant. While such an expert can arrogantly believe that PME practice has been entirely absent until his or her arrival, we know that no organisation is

without a PME system in one form or another, however embryonic, informal, or poorly documented. We suggest here that, for the sake of ownership, effectiveness and sustainability, our role is to build on what already exists, however fragmentary, to recognise strengths and to strive at all times for practicality and simplicity: effectiveness and cost-consciousness should displace PME overkill.

WHO IS THIS BOOK FOR AND HOW CAN IT BE USED?

Who did we have in mind when writing this book? In the first place, PME facilitators, who might be working individually, with non-governmental organisations (NGOs) or consultancy companies to support civil society organisations engaged in development work (see Box 1.2). The cases we describe reflect our work with such organisations, whether faith-based, community-based, or loosely referred to as NGOs.

Box 1.2 This Book has been Written for...

✓ PME facilitators and trainers supporting civil society organisations.
✓ PME practitioners and coaches working within these organisations, or as consultants.
✓ Other PME users, such as desk officers with donor agencies.

This volume will be of interest to others too: we offer a varied menu, of use to PME coaches and mentors, and to PME users who will read about other experiences and practical tips and obtain better support to meet their PME needs. This book is, however, not meant to address PME beginners' needs and it is not a manual: we do not offer a blueprint, with a series of steps to be rigidly followed. Much rather, we hope to inspire would-be PME facilitators and to stimulate reflection and innovation.

Donor agency staff and other development workers might also be interested to read these pages: with them we hope to enrich dialogue and to influence practice, so that better PME support becomes available. What is suggested here may require from all of us, including donors and other actors, more flexible approaches than has hitherto been the case. Our collective learning capacity, essential for building trust and good relationships with partners, can often be improved.

Throughout this volume, we use real-life examples from our practice, to illustrate some of the points made in the main text, although we have changed names where confidentiality demanded it. These have been presented in boxes with a distinctive icon ('*Notes*') and have summaries of what we consider, again from our experience, useful tips for PME facilitators.

This book consists of nine chapters, arranged into three main parts. We encourage the reader to select areas of interest: there is no need to read this volume from cover to cover! In Part 1, 'Why Are We Here?', we have explored the book's rationale (Chapter 1). We also focus on the language used in PME practice, the confusion that this often leads to and we propose a few working definitions (Chapter 2).

In Part 2, 'Bringing PME into Daily Practice', Chapter 3 suggests how a 'total organisation approach', as defined earlier, can be facilitated to good effect. It also discusses how we can help partner organisations better appreciate that PME, rather than donor conditionality, can make life easier and improve on the impact they want to make. Chapters 4 and 5 explore what is needed at the organisational level for effective PME, with a focus on learning in Chapter 5. Chapter 6 examines how influences beyond the boundaries of the organisation, such as those of donors and of national culture need to be dealt with.

In Part 3, 'Further Customising PME', Chapter 7 outlines ways to adapt PME processes and systems to fit diverse organisational characteristics, needs, skills and types (such as smaller community-based organisations, or mature faith-based organisations). In Chapter 8, we share our PME facilitation experiences with partner organisations involved in advocacy, emergency situations, or capacity-building. It also discusses how we can facilitate the type of PME process that this implies. Chapter 9 sums up how we can plan, implement and evaluate such a process, as well as the requisite attitude which we, as PME facilitators, might want to adhere to. To conclude, we offer an annotated bibliography for those who may wish to read more about PME, for *proving and improving.*

2

PME: WATCHING WORDS AND MEANINGS

Clarity of concepts and words is essential when facilitating PME processes. Our story from Cambodia (see Box 2.1) illustrates how confusion can arise when practitioners from different cultural and language backgrounds meet and work. With 'PME speak', even resorting to a dictionary may be of little help. In this chapter, we share experiences and tips on a good start, clarifying terms and rising above the war of words.

DEVELOPMENT SPEAK VERSUS REAL LANGUAGE

While some development workers are very particular about terminology, others understand terms as used in day-to-day life. The gap widens as development jargon spreads: 'reviews' become 'revisits', but then is 'revisiting a concept' different from 'viewing it again'? Perhaps, but is it worthwhile to look for such

Box 2.1 Confusion Across Cultures: A Near-fiasco in Cambodia

A foreign trainer had come to guide the staff of a national NGO on result-based management. While the participants could understand some English, they depended to a great extent on the translation provided by their colleagues. The trainer, in trying to explain the difference between 'output' and 'outcome', described 'output' as a result achieved during the project period and 'outcome' as the end of project result. After much discussion on this, the trainer felt frustrated by the participants' apparent inability to understand the two terms. Further effort, ice-breaking exercises and examples were thrown in. Frustration grew: the participants insisted they understood, but the looks on their faces told a different story. The day ended on this note.

The next day began with a recap. Several participants owned up: the difference between 'output' and 'outcome' was not clear. There was an air of dejection in the room. Further exploration, however, alerted the trainer to the fact that the words 'outcome' and 'output' were translated using the definitions and examples given, yet in the local Khmer language, only one word—'latephal' or 'result'—was available. This had led to much confusion and irritation, which could now be overcome.

The facilitator from then on made sure she would guard participants against trying to find dictionary translations. PME work has its own, often confusing, language, much like 'computer speak'.

shades of difference? Our experience as PME facilitators warns us of possible confusion, as the different languages, interpretations and backgrounds of community residents, development workers and others intermingle. Further confusion arises in the minds of development practitioners when the same words are used and explained differently by us, the PME facilitators. Workshop participants then appear bemused and protest that a previous trainer introduced 'outputs' differently, but equally convincingly. In our experience, there is often confusion about the following terms:

1. **Monitoring and evaluation:** Why do some visitors call their annual tour a 'monitoring visit' and others an 'evaluation'? It is rarely explained that both may be looking at things from equally valid perspectives. For the former, the visit takes place when a project is ongoing, to suggest mid-course corrections. For the latter, a one-year term is ending and there is an opportunity to look back and identify areas of strengths, learning and improvements. Confusion also arises when only 'evaluation' is said to lead to future corrections and changes, whereas 'monitoring' is confined to 'collecting and reviewing information' (see Box 2.2). Evaluation is also at times—wrongly—defined as meeting information needs for consumption outside the implementing organisation, whereas monitoring is inward-looking. Both monitoring and evaluation need to cross these artificial boundaries.

2. **Results:** Different interpretations here also lead to confusion, even conflict. In the NGO world, some see 'results' as a source of pride for accomplishments, or as necessary to learn whether objectives are being reached. Others see 'results' as needed to convince donors to continue their support; yet others decry the use of 'results' as originating from the profit-seeking business world, or (as in 'result-based management') used to describe an organisational focus on results as the main benchmark for effectiveness. These different perceptions are complicated by uncertainty as to whether results are being considered at the level of 'outputs', 'effects', 'outcomes', or 'impacts'.

3. **Activity, output, outcome, effect:** Some define 'outputs' as 'the goods and services delivered', or 'results at the production level', such as wells drilled as part of a water programme. Others as 'immediate change' at the beneficiary level, or 'results at the utilisation level' (people begin to use well water). Another

Box 2.2 P, M and E: Working Definitions

There are many definitions of planning, monitoring and evaluation, just as they are a wide variety of development organisations using PME in different ways. In this book, we look at PME as *a way of doing*, even a *way of thinking* about what an organisation wants to achieve and the planning, monitoring and evaluation practices it needs in order to do so: *what* to achieve (plan), *how* is it reaching this (monitoring) and *why* it is going the way it is (evaluating).

Planning (whether 'operational', 'strategic', 'project-based') normally involves thinking before an action about its 'why' (the objective), what (the activities), how (the approach and strategy), when and where, with whom and by whom, and with what resources.

Monitoring and *evaluation* both aim at assessing change and at being as efficient and effective as possible in bringing about (or contributing to) this change. Monitoring and evaluation both focus on learning from successes and shortcomings and on establishing accountability. They are therefore often mentioned together, although *monitoring* focuses on ongoing surveillance or assessment of an initiative.

Monitoring helps to gauge the degree of achievement of activities, whether resources have been well utilised and whether one is on course towards achieving results. One can then learn from this, celebrate success and make corrections where needed.

Evaluation, on the other hand, focuses on changes that can normally be seen after some time. It helps to find out if results have been achieved, whether there is any impact, whether strategy and approach were appropriate, whether there have been any unanticipated changes and the reasons for any variations from a plan. One can then learn from successes and failures, make corrections (in approaches, goals, programmes and macro strategies) where necessary and, of course, celebrate successes too!

interpretation of output and outcome is time-related: either as immediate results, achieved during the project, or as results that must be achieved at the end of it. There is also much confusion when these terms are used to manipulate logframes.

4. **Indicators:** These are also the subject of much debate and experience suggests that PME beginners often identify indicators

as an important learning need. Thus, when asked for an indicator for 'increased income', common answers are 'increases in household assets', or 'investment in children's education'. While some facilitators will agree, others will say that such indicators have a cause–effect, or an outcome–impact relationship: how can

Box 2.3 Two Ways of Presenting Indicators in Relation to Objectives

The existence of two schools of thought in presenting indicators, in combination with a particular way of describing objectives, arose at a workshop in Rwanda. This example shows that the necessary information is provided using either option, but presentation differs. The first option might be preferable, as it describes objectives in terms of a desirable (and feasible) final situation, instead of using the rather vague descriptions in the second option. The first option also avoids preconceived values for indicators, in favour of neutral terms.

Option 1		Option 2	
Intervention Logic	Indicators	Intervention Logic	Indicators
Overall objective: Morbidity level reduced by 15% in village X.	Impact indicators: • Morbidity level.	Overall objective: Contribute to healthcare provision.	Impact indicators: • Morbidity level lowered by 15% in village X.
Specific objective: Operational health cooperative with 90 members and a financial turnover of $ 360, handling 75% of health cases within 3 years.	Effect indicators: • Number of members. • Financial turnover. • Level of satisfaction. • Number of cases handled.	Specific objective: Contribute to the creation of an effective health cooperative.	Effect indicators: • Health cooperative with 90 members and financial turnover of $ 360. • At least 75% of patients satisfied with services.

Our experience shows that this presentation helps to describe the two 'schools', their inter-changeability and to select the preferred option, depending on level of comfort and possibly donor preference.

the impact (higher-level result) be the indicator of the outcome (lower-level result)? Another source of confusion with indicators arises from different ways of presenting them, such as whether they should include targets (90 per cent of children immunised) (see Box 2.3).

IMPLICATIONS FOR THE FACILITATOR

Many of these definitions have their logic and can convince the learner. But let us spare a thought for those unfortunate PME users who interact with two consultants sent by two donors in a single month, who speak different languages with total conviction, often dismissing the interpretation of the other 'expert'.

CLARIFYING TERMS

As facilitators, what can we do to reassure our partners? We can first share a few working definitions (see Box 2.4). We propose the following, in full knowledge that others exist and are equally valid:

1. **A results hierarchy**. PME is about making a change and thus *achieving results*: given the importance attached to the word 'result', a common understanding is essential. Equally important, and easily shown, is that we deal with different (often three) levels of results. In this hierarchy, results at one level (the outputs) are necessary for achieving results at the next level (the outcomes, or effects) and outcomes contribute significantly to the expected results at the third level (impact).

2. **Output** can be explained as what a project *produces* to be used by 'beneficiaries'. It is a 'first level result', arising from a combination of activities, using the required *inputs* (human and other resources). At this level, an individual project may thus undergo an *efficiency assessment*, examining its implementation in terms of quality, quantity and cost. These can be judged against *benchmarks*, or targets. Output monitoring, apart from ways to allocate all costs to an output, is generally fairly easy to conduct and we often find that partner organisations have appropriate systems for this.

Box 2.4 Clarifying PME Terms

✓ Helping to develop a common understanding of 'results' within a partner organisation, using examples from local practice, is a useful task for the facilitator at the outset of a PME support process.

✓ As facilitators, we may enhance this understanding by reviewing the linkages between different result levels. This could take the form of a ladder, with each rung representing a result level: the question 'Why?' helps to climb the ladder towards 'impact' level, the question 'How?' to descend it towards 'activity' level.

✓ Partner organisations often find PME beyond the output level challenging: at the outset of a process, we can help explain why this is so and to start a discussion on the need to move beyond this level in PME practice.

✓ Comparing terminology to reassure: this overview of terms used by different agencies provides a useful tool to demonstrate the three result levels and the confusing terminology used.

Agency	3rd level results	2nd level results	1st level results
CARE	Final goal	Intermediate goals	Outputs
DANIDA	Development objective	Immediate objectives	Outputs
EU	Overall objectives	Project purpose	Expected results
GTZ	Overall goal	Project purpose	Results/outputs
UN Agencies	Impact	Effect	Outputs
USAID	Final goal	Strategic goal	Intermediate results
World Bank	Goal	Project purpose	Outputs

This encourages our partners in their struggle to come to grips with terminology: these terms are inter-changeable and there is no single correct definition. Further, the terminology presented in this table, as accepted by each agency in 1997, may have changed several times since then.

3. **Outcome (or effect)** constitutes the second level in our results hierarchy and describes how the beneficiary has *used* the outputs. Outcomes normally have quantitative and qualitative aspects. It may take some time (a season, even several years) for full outcomes

to become visible, although traces may appear early on. An outcome will also largely depend on the original problem analysis for which, say, an activity has been identified as crucial to tackle the desired change. There will generally be a fairly direct cause–effect relation between outputs and outcomes: as organisations learn from past experiences, they will know that certain outputs are likely to produce certain outcomes.

At this second level, an *effectiveness* evaluation will focus on the question: 'To what extent have the outputs been effective to achieve the intended outcomes?' We will therefore ask: 'How did the beneficiary utilise the products or services?' and 'How did this application contribute to achieving the objective of a particular programme?' Measuring outcomes is then not only about measuring the total outcome of a programme: it may also entail measuring the outcome of each separate activity to arrive, for instance, at the most effective combination of activities. Questions might then include: 'Are some activities more effective than others? Are some superfluous? Must some be added?' In our experience, few development organisations have effective outcome monitoring systems, although they often have much informal knowledge about outcomes.

4. **Impact** mostly refers to desired change in the long term. This might result from the collective effort of several actors, such as governments and NGOs, each contributing to impact, rather than achieving it single-handedly. As for outcomes, impact is also about measuring the *contribution* that an individual programme has made in achieving the overall objective. Again, this may help the organisation to review and change the current mix of programmes to achieve greater impact with fewer resources. As with outcomes, it may take years before full impact becomes visible, but once the beneficiary starts *using* the outputs, leading to certain effects, the first traces of impact should become visible.

At the impact level, cause–effect relations are usually neither clear nor very direct as a number of other factors and actors may have an influence. In practice, it therefore may not often make sense to try and evaluate the impact of one individual project on, say, the quality of life of poor people. Nevertheless, to foresee impact is of great importance to an organisation's strategy and thinking. An organisation, having learned from past experiences, may be able to estimate whether its programmes have at least contributed to impact. In our experience, few organisations have effective impact monitoring systems, although they may have some informal information about this. There is often a tendency to avoid impact measurement, because it is seen as a long-term and complex affair, or because (as is often the case) the desired impact is overambitious.

THE NATURE OF CHANGE

One debate among development practitioners concerns the nature of change. Critics of the logframe, for instance, say it encourages a perception of change as linear and predictable. Yet, one can perceive change differently, often with rather unpredictable results. Promoting an understanding of change and the various ways in which it manifests itself can help in the PME facilitation process. This may, for instance, include recognising that there are circumstances where an intervention is surrounded by uncertainty in spite of very rigorous planning, or where one needs to constantly adapt to bring about the intended change, or where innovation and unplanned work is desirable. This can help build an understanding of what effective PME processes are and the challenges this presents. Keeping eye and mind open to unintended as well as intended outcomes and impacts is part of this: these can be crucial for planning, re-planning and ultimate success. We return to this issue in later chapters.

WHO IS THE EXPERT?

Given this uncertainty and these debates, it is best to avoid presenting ourselves as experts, whose perspective and definitions are 'the only right ones'. Is it indeed not better to acknowledge diversity and to embrace it? So let us be clear, concise and avoid complex words. Let us also remember that the end result of PME is not about clarity of terminology, but about effective learning and accountability (see Box 2.5).

Box 2.5 Who is the Expert?

✓ Whenever possible, let us select the words that best fit the context (culture, language, educational levels) and objectives of a particular process. English, Spanish, or French equivalents are sometimes clearer to all than clumsy translations. Synonyms can also help to demystify terms. Thus, for 'results', we can use 'success', 'what motivates us', 'what gives us pride'. We can also elaborate the concept of 'result' by using a key activity, or real-life example from an existing programme.

✓ We can also briefly explain the advantages and drawbacks of terms mentioned by participants. This avoids spending excessive time on definitions at the expense of progress on more important matters.

✓ We can then build consensus around one set of definitions, stressing that these are not necessarily the only correct ones to describe PME concepts. Although we may also wish to refer, if need be, to the definitions proposed in this chapter, criticising other facilitators' definitions generally wastes time.

✓ Ownership of a PME process can be built by involving as many of the stakeholders of an organisation as possible in this consensus and reconciliation, so all agree on one set of definitions without finding fault with each other.

3

A TOTAL ORGANISATION
APPROACH TO PME

We mentioned the need for 'a total organisation approach' to PME, a need to go beyond PME linked to programmes, or projects, or even 'only' with achieving results for the 'beneficiaries'. Such an approach takes into consideration the organisations' environment, its partners and competitors, in a context informed, among other factors, by local and national cultures. It also takes into account important organisational dimensions, including the financial dimension. This chapter outlines why such an approach is, in our view, necessary, what it entails and how it can be facilitated.

WHY FACILITATE A 'TOTAL ORGANISATION' APPROACH TO PME?

A total organisational approach to PME reflects our belief that strong organisations are essential for sustained development

The link between programme-PME and organisation-wide PME is logical. Management and staff can quickly see that programme-based PME does not stand isolated, but is part of wider organisational PME. All staff at all levels are already involved in regular M&E practices, from drivers, secretaries and field workers to management. If management acknowledges this, it becomes an important indicator for the overall appreciation of the role of PME in the organisation.

A first informal meeting with the Teso Diocese Planning and Development Office (TEDDO), a Ugandan NGO, focused on the assessment of their current PME practices. Invitations were left to the TEDDO management and everyone was asked to attend. Drivers, storekeepers, secretaries, field extension workers, programme coordinators, the director, board members—all were present. This demonstrated a recognition of PME as part and parcel of each person's job or task, each contributing to the progress of the organisation.

and that an organisation is more than the sum of the projects it implements (see Box 3.1). Yet, in practice, we often see PME limited to the management of individual (often donor-funded) projects.

We can summarise our approach by asking the question: 'What is a strong organisation?' instead of the more limited: 'What is an effective project or programme?' To answer this, we can identify three familiar dimensions of an organisation of any size or type: its *being, doing* and *relating,* to which a fourth, *learning,* can be added, making up a four-circle model. A clear *vision/mission* links these dimensions and steers their development.

When we think of an organisation that way, we see that a strong programme (the 'doing') not only arises because of good design and sustained results, but also because it is supported by a powerful vision, clear long-term objectives and strategies, by an effective organisation with adequate resources and by strong working relations with others. If all these components are effective and support each other, we are likely to have an effective organisation. We have found that the four-circle (or similar) model (see Further Reading) can help others understand why PME has to look beyond programmes to entire organisations and contextual issues, to find reasons for strengths and weaknesses and identify where actions might be required. Practice indeed shows that meaningful indicators for strong organisations are found not only in the *doing,* but also in the other dimensions.

To achieve its overall vision/mission, an organisation must therefore pay attention to (*a*) the development of a vision/mission for its beneficiaries, (*b*) its own development as an organisation, (*c*) its context and the selection of context-related strategies and (*d*) financial information and management. We suggest here that a total organisational approach to PME must do likewise and make the same linkages. PME support thus includes several organisational aspects although in adopting such an approach we do not strive to change an entire organisation, but to understand which factors are most important to achieve organisational objectives, and thus help it determine which PME systems and practices best support these objectives (see Box 3.2).

> **Box 3.2 Introducing a 'Total Organisation Approach to PME'**
>
> ✓ The four-circle organisational model ('doing', 'relating', 'being', 'learning') can help others understand why PME must 'look' beyond programmes to organisational components to find reasons for strengths and weaknesses, and identify where actions might be required (see Further Reading, IC Consults' organisational scans).
>
> ✓ Sketching a partner's organogramme can also help to quickly explain the total organisational approach. This clarifies how different functions (persons, departments) within an organisation generate information flows: project or programme-related PME takes into account information on finance and administration, human resources and management, which also monitors the context. Some of these flows are more formal than others, but a decision will tend to reflect all this information.
>
> ✓ Involving as many staff, including 'junior' staff, and other stakeholders as possible will also help. This may need encouragement, depending on organisational culture, and may start with discussions that directly concern their tasks.

BEYOND INDIVIDUAL PROJECT OR PROGRAMME

An effective organisation needs to consciously select and implement projects or programmes that reflect its vision and mission for its 'beneficiaries'. This presupposes that even when the focus is on a particular project or programme, the mission of the organisation for its beneficiaries also needs to be explored and how particular activities and programmes contribute to its realisation. These are strategic choices, which, if poor, will prove later not to have been 'effective'.

As facilitators, we can help with such programme selection (or its review) during strategic planning sessions. Two facilitation issues often arise here: first, where projects have a funding ceiling, or limited life span (often three years), and have to fit in a wider programme that was chosen to make a strategic contribution to the achievement of the vision and mission. Second, where

Box 3.3 More than Just a Collection of Projects—Shantir Neer's 'Porganogramme'

Shantir Neer implements several projects for women's empowerment and child development in western Bangladesh. As with many other NGOs, its activities are planned and implemented project by project. Staff are recruited for specific projects, according to project organogrammes.

With a growing number of projects, Shantir Neer's director decided to shift from project-based to organisation-wide planning to enhance coherence. With suggestions from friends and experts, the director started clustering project activities to develop an overall programme framework, whose management required a new consolidated organogramme for Shantir Neer as a whole.

To do this, the director copied and collated the organogrammes of various projects. This led to a complicated management structure, which he found very difficult to handle, and which was soon jokingly referred to as Shantir Neer's project-based organogramme or 'porganogramme'. Outside help was eventually sought to develop an effective organisational organogramme.

funding requirements lead a development organisation to make compromises in the selection of projects. Some projects are then chosen because funds are forthcoming, rather than as necessary to achieve the vision and mission, a situation exacerbated when strategic planning exercises are not undertaken. These points are discussed in the next chapters.

The call to go beyond the level of managing projects/ programmes can be summarised as the need for organisational focus, where all projects contribute to the achievement of what the organisation stands for. We have found it useful to include this *focus* message in our PME facilitation: if there is no focus in what the organisation is doing and trying to achieve, then PME loses much of its justification (see Boxes 3.4 and 3.5).

Box 3.4 Keeping Focus among NGOs in Papua New Guinea

When asked how they could improve their PME practice, the staff of NGOs in Papua New Guinea found this a difficult and abstract question. To help answer it, the perspective of an overall organisation was adopted. This helped them to quickly discover that all elements of PME were not only part and parcel of their own operations, within their own organisations, but also in their own communities. The focus of the organisations, good leadership and team spirit were identified as most important factors for good PME practice.

The focus of the organisation emerged as the combination of three aspects: (a) always looking for sound and sustainable results ('serving the people'), (b) a clear description of the relations with others in the environment and (c) the quality of the work itself. It was also agreed that without this clear focus it makes little sense to design a PME system. The entire organisation needs to have a good focus to which all projects or programmes contribute. Such focus was indeed seen as a driving force for PME that is not only project or programme-related.

INCLUDING A VISION AND MISSION FOR THE DEVELOPMENT OF THE ORGANISATION

As facilitators, we also often need to emphasise that the achievement of long-term objectives for the beneficiary group will at some stage be at risk if the organisation fails to develop or functions sub-optimally. The organisation therefore needs to consciously select programmes and activities to achieve the objectives set for its own development. For a total organisation approach, both types of programmes and objectives (at the beneficiary and organisational levels) therefore need to be planned, monitored and evaluated. We then again see that PME must capture information that allows evaluative judgements to be made beyond operational or project levels (see Box 3.6).

Box 3.6 Reflection Questions Linked to Achieving Vision/ Mission and Objectives at the Organisation Level

✓ As facilitators, we can use a second set of questions to trigger reflection on meeting the vision/mission of the partner organisation itself.

  • Is the mission still relevant? Does it need updating?
  • What progress has been made in becoming a sustainable organisation?
  • How can capacities and resources be assessed and developed to strengthen the organisation? What organisation structure can optimise results and bring synergy? How can all staff contribute to the overall organisation goal?
  • What kind of culture would fit the organisation and how can it move towards it? Is it all-inclusive? How can gender be mainstreamed into the organisation and work monitored accordingly?
  • How does the PME system operate? Is the PME policy still appropriate? Does PME contribute to learning, better accountability and higher effectiveness?

✓ Such questions are relevant to all types of development organisations, whatever their degree of maturity. We can, however, explain that all these cannot be answered by a PME system that is only linked to programmes or projects, pointing to the need for organisation-wide PME.

WHERE IS THE LOST COUSIN? FINANCIAL PME AS PART OF THE OVERALL PME

Ensuring that financial information is available for effective evaluations at output, outcome and impact levels, and at both project/programme and organisational levels, is often a neglected aspect of PME. In such a situation, narrative and financial reporting is not integrated and a full-fledged evaluation cannot take place.

For PME at these different levels, the organisation must have financial objectives, strategies and policies, such as a good internal control system, plans to achieve financial sustainability, having a transparent cost-allocation system and the like. All these belong to the territory of what we may call 'financial PME'. As a facilitator, it is useful to stress that financial PME should facilitate the planning, monitoring and evaluation of activities, projects and programmes and must thus provide financial information in the two distinct areas we are now familiar with: (*a*) PME of activities and programmes, evaluating cost-efficiency and effectiveness and (*b*) PME of important financial policies, objectives and strategies for the effective functioning of the organisation itself (see Box 3.7).

> ### Box 3.7 Reflection Questions for Financial PME
>
> ✓ For financial PME, the practical evaluation questions might include:
>
> - Has this output been delivered efficiently and cost-effectively?
> - Is this programme cost-efficient and cost-effective?
> - How cost-effective is each programme in achieving the organisation's overall objectives?
>
> ✓ To answer such questions, we may need to facilitate steps towards the adoption of:
>
> - An activity-based accounting system (to allocate costs to the correct activities within particular projects, or programmes).
> - A transparent cost-allocation system (to allocate all costs, including overheads, to the strategic activities of the organisation).
> - Participatory result-oriented budgeting, involving all staff in the organisation.
>
> We return to these in more detail in Chapter 5.

BEYOND THE ORGANISATION AND ITS PROGRAMMES

More than ever before, development organisations work in a context where other actors and institutions, including governments and private businesses, also operate. Even within a single sector, such as education or health, different actors enjoy different degrees of power and play various roles, sometimes complementary, sometimes in competition. As facilitators, we often find ourselves helping partner organisations keep track of, and maintain relations with, these actors. Effective organisations also need to monitor changes in the social, economic and political factors that shape this environment and influence their performance, thus recognising that project/programme results are affected by forces outside their control.

It is therefore important that an organisation makes a sound 'landscape analysis' and reflects on (*a*) its *positioning* in its environment among other key development actors, (*b*) its strategic *relevance* in terms of its chosen programmes and main activities and (*c*) how it intends *to work with* important (non-beneficiary) actors, for instance, to ensure sustained benefits after a programme has come to an end (see Box 3.8).

We have found that many organisations neglect to undertake regular, formal landscape analyses, thus threatening their relevance, effectiveness and reputation. Without such an analysis (and this is

Box 3.8 Reflection Questions on Achieving a Strong Position in the Context

✓ If we consider the wider context as PME facilitators, reflection questions could include:

- Does the organisation assess external factors/assumptions? How does it assess external relationships?
- To what extent can results (especially impacts) be attributed to a project/programme, or to contextual factors?
- How does the organisation appreciate and keep track of relevant government policies/donor policies?
- How do other organisations in the environment perform? Is the organisation as cost-effective as other actors engaged in similar programmes?
- Can collaboration with other actors be enhanced? Does the organisation learn from others, develop and share practices? With whom can joint advocacy take place?
- How can collaboration better lead to sustained change? How does the organisation empower beneficiaries to engage with other actors?

✓ We can again point out that such questions cannot be answered by project- or programme-based PME only, thus underlining the need for 'a total organisational approach to PME'.

where learning is often problematic), we often see an organisation committing itself to a vision/mission and long-term objectives that are either irrelevant to the beneficiaries, or prove to be beyond its capacity. Where they do keep a close watch, contextual information is mostly collected on an informal basis. As facilitators, we should emphasise that PME not only deals with the *operational* aspects of activities, projects and programmes, it must also test the assumptions that have been made in adopting these strategies, policies, or programmes. Ultimately, the organisation may even question its long-term objectives and vision/mission because of changes in the wider context and incorporate this in its PME practice. We return to contextual analysis in Chapter 6.

4

GETTING PME GOING WITHIN THE ORGANISATION

Having defined our total organisational approach to PME, we can now turn to putting intentions in practice, first by looking at ways to help organisations meet internal requirements. This chapter highlights some generic issues (faced by many organisations). It focuses on common facilitation challenges and possible ways to overcome them, as the PME cycle unfolds, as well as on the organisational resources and structures necessary for PME work.

THE FIRST STEPS: THREE QUESTIONS

We begin by recognising that a good understanding of PME and its terminology is not sufficient for PME to be accepted in the organisation as part of daily practice, with all concerned *owning* and *participating* in it. Yet this is essential to turn PME into a tool for self-assessment and internal learning. Only then will *all* reflect on past experience, examine present realities, revisit objectives and define future strategies, recognising the different needs of stakeholders and negotiating their diverse claims and interests. The PME process then also becomes flexible, adapting to local contexts and constantly changing circumstances.

PME FOR WHAT?

We sometimes find partner organisations reacting towards PME by distancing themselves from it, or seeing it as an imposition. Indeed, PME can evoke fears, real, or imagined: the fear of having one's mistakes exposed, of seeing one's authority undermined, of having to spend large resources in time and money, of being all too complicated. Yet, why is PME relevant to development organisations? This question can constitute a first step to reconcile with PME and to embrace it as good for organisational health. It may well be the most critical step in establishing an effective PME process.

Partner organisations often see upward accountability for funds and results (usually to donors, or governments) as an essential function of their PME systems. This is often at the expense of 'downward' accountability to the beneficiaries that organisations exist to serve, or to 'subordinate' staff whose personal responsibility for results we want to encourage. This view is closely entwined with culture: it may not be easy for a 'boss' to feel accountable to his or her staff; or to help beneficiaries critically comment on the performance of an organisation that claims to work for their good. What is even more difficult sometimes is 'lateral' accountability: when competition between development organisations for funding, status and recognition is intense, sharing information does not come naturally, even across sections, or departments within a single organisation. An organisation then needs help to tackle such barriers to learning, so that it can become a responsible partner in development and acquires the self-confidence needed to avoid being inward-looking, or constrained by business-like competitive behaviour.

How then can we review essential PME functions? First, a PME system that stresses accountability highlights an important function,

PME for proving. Performing such a function is frequently reflected in detailed planning and elaborate M&E procedures, often prompted by elaborate donor, or government reporting requirements, such as demands for many indicators and large sample sizes which can be statistically analysed. Such rigour can make development organisations feel better in control although, where elaborate PME systems have to rely on a few staff with the required skills, wider participation within the organisation becomes difficult. Rigour can also require much time and resources, as when formal external evaluations involve consultants checking on progress and measuring impact. In spite of such constraints, having to prove, first to oneself as a team, and then to others (beneficiaries, governments, donors) to enhance credibility and retain their confidence, is often essential.

A PME system can also put emphasis on learning: *PME for improving.* This entails capturing information to learn, learning from this and applying the lessons learnt. While this seems quite straightforward, it can require quite a change in practice. Yet, without learning, what organisation can hope to survive in an ever faster changing and competitive environment? Partner organisations thus need help to create every possible opportunity for learning, for themselves and their beneficiaries. By knowing one has contributed to making a change, by being ready to accept mistakes (and learn from them), PME for improving can also help build self-confidence and effectiveness at individual, team and organisational levels.

A focus on improving leads us to look at PME somewhat differently. A small sample size with key indicators, enabling the organisation to repeat M&E exercises regularly and to use a more participatory approach, can, for instance, be sufficient to yield a plausible picture of a situation, highlighting key trends. The challenge is to make informal learning more legitimate, visible and systematic, keeping an 'improving' focus in mind when doing so. When planning, we can also adopt a light approach (detailed during the first year and indicative for the next years, for example) with the expectation that M&E will provide the necessary feedback to refine later plans (see Box 4.1).

PME for proving and for improving are two different, but complementary functions: we can account for results and thus learn. One function is more outward looking, the other (learning) more directly concerned with the 'self' (although too much navel-gazing

Box 4.1 Proving or Improving: An Indian Story

Accion Fraterna (AF), a large Indian NGO, has been implementing a soil and water conservation programme in drought-stricken hills to improve rain-fed agriculture for poor farmers. This includes the construction of *bunds* (earthen terraces to check runoff and control erosion).

Three years on, an internal evaluation revealed that farmers had ploughed over a third of the *bunds*. AF regretted this, but subsequent consultations with farmers revealed sound technical reasons for the 'sabotage'. Farmers could not cope with contours running over their small fields, dividing them in portions that were difficult to plough. They preferred terraces on their field boundaries, which also proved effective in controlling erosion. AF therefore changed its design and planning to accommodate farmers' preferences.

This experience taught AF that farmers have sound technical skills that could complement those of engineers at the planning stage and that, in spite of its learning culture, AF had lost valuable money, time and labour by not having timely evaluation mechanisms. One way to rectify this was to involve the 'beneficiaries' in M&E to deepen AF's learning.

This PME experience improved AF's health. It also showed that M&E aims at reducing wastage of resources. Instead of being expensive, as often thought, it can save money.

is to be avoided). We highlight both functions to help organisations decide how to strike the right balance between them. Each function will be associated with the use of certain approaches, tools and techniques although here too organisations have a tendency to assimilate PME tools only with those, such as logframes and specific, measurable, achievable, relevant, time-bound (SMART) indicators, used for accountability purposes.

Finally, by using *PME for relating* in a multi-actor context, an organisation can learn and improve, raise its profile and strengthen its legitimacy and reputation. It can also be helped to think of linked PME systems, examining, for instance, whether parts of a donor PME system can fit with its own, without compromising its independence, checking on divergent, or common interests, and where these meet in practice. PME is then associated with partnerships, levels of trust, accountability, integrity and openness: from this perspective, organisations may then also need help in using PME to develop and maintain healthy relationships.

How about a PME Policy?

The rationale for PME can usefully be summarised in a policy document, which does not have to be weighty, especially for a small organisation, where one page may suffice, so long as it refers to the total organisation (whatever its size) and not to a particular project. Such a policy may refer to a strategic level (the why) and an operational one (the how). We may need to suggest such a policy, once the organisation has a good grasp of the basics of PME.

We have found that the need for a PME policy often emerges when an organisation is confronted with different donors, or government departments, each with their own reporting and other requirements, that is, when an organisation finds matching its PME needs with those of external parties difficult. It is also the time when it realises that clarity becomes necessary, as to the importance of PME for itself, what it embraces and what is needed (money, skills) to make it effective. We believe that our task as facilitators is to emphasise that the organisation's requirements must take precedence and occupy the heart of its PME system. A facilitator must therefore help clarify these internal needs first. Once they have been well understood, they are often easier to match with external requirements than one would have anticipated (see Box 4.2).

The development of a PME policy calls for varying processes, depending on the organisation. A network may need discussions involving all its members. In a small organisation, all stakeholders can quickly lay a common foundation. In a mid-size organisation, a review of current PME practice may be necessary before developing or reviewing a policy. A large organisation may also need a review, as well as perspective building if a feeling has developed that, say, 'M&E is nothing but policing'. Bureaucratic organisations, large or small, may require more hand-holding to break deeply anchored attitudes in implementing a PME policy. A facilitator may then initially organise meetings to demonstrate an alternative model,

Box 4.2 Developing a PME Policy

✓ To develop a PME policy, a clear understanding of the basics of PME, its rationale and terminology is needed. We may have to help a partner organisation in this respect and to link this understanding to its information needs, clarifying a useful balance between 'PME for proving' and 'PME for improving'.

✓ Emphasising that learning takes place at both individual and organisational levels, that PME needs to be planned and budgeted for and that PME needs to be part of daily operations and practice for everyone in the organisation are also important at this stage.

✓ Reflecting a total organisation approach, the linkages between PME for a particular project, or programme, and the entire organisation may need emphasising.

✓ A PME policy also needs its own M&E. A common reflection on the various aspects of PME practice to see whether they really add to the quality of learning and implementation is useful. Relevant questions might include: How much time is spent on PME and is it worth the effort? Does the information collected generate knowledge and wisdom? Are all indicators still relevant? Are sample sizes and frequencies still adequate? Are different roles and responsibilities still appropriate? Are skills sufficient?

but later take a backseat and provide feedback to those concerned (see Box 4.3).

DOES PME NEED PLANNING TOO?

The answer may be an obvious 'yes', yet little attention is generally paid to planning PME itself. After clarifying the objectives of PME, and the balance between PME for proving and for improving, the following questions are pertinent: 'At what levels and how frequently do planning and budgeting need to take place? What must be monitored for whom, for what and by whom? Who will be responsible for the various steps of the PME process and what will be their roles? Will the beneficiary group be involved? How will information be collected, collated and analysed? What will be the feedback mechanisms? How will learning be facilitated? How will

Box 4.3 Establishing a Sound Foundation for PME

When I facilitate an introductory workshop on PME, I include a session on basic rationale: 'Why do we do PME?' I often start with the Indian story about building anti-erosion terraces and the farmers ploughing over them (see Box 4.1). Participants are then asked to reflect and share similar stories from their own experiences. This usually yields successes, challenges and learning points. With further discussion on the reasons for any failure, one gets a picture of the quality of learning in the organisation, the richness of informal knowledge and organisational dynamics.

This, however, requires going beyond immediate answers. People tend to respond to questions such as 'What is PME?' and 'Why do you do PME?' by referring to deviations from work plans, targets and budgets, which need to be checked and corrected. If we insist, however (such as by asking the question 'So what?'), staff start to mention PME as necessary to answer deeper reflection needs in the organisation and learning to better deliver sustained results for the target group.

Story telling is therefore a useful tool to identify possible entry points and obstacles for further work. It vividly illustrates the total organisation approach, as it highlights aspects of the organisation and its context which affect learning quality and capacity. Using such information openly, the organisation enhances awareness of its weak and strong points and becomes better able to receive sometimes unpleasant or critical messages.

the PME system itself be monitored and evaluated?' It is during the planning phase that different stakeholders of the organisation need to come together to articulate their concerns and agree on differing interests, and own a comprehensive PME plan.

PLANNING ISSUES

As facilitators, we have frequently met a number of challenges with regard to the 'P' of PME: fuzziness in specifying objectives and indicators, reluctance to think strategically and to make the connections with day-to-day operations, being overambitious, handling logframes and marginalising the budgeting process.

We look at these in turn, while keeping in mind the nature, age and size of the organisation being helped to set up, or review a planning framework. A young, growing organisation may, for instance, need frequent strategic decision-making workshops with the involvement of as many stakeholders as possible. This frequency may reduce for mid-size or larger organisations. In larger, better established organisations and in networks, the process may be more elaborate and involve the participation of different stakeholders at different times. Plans may also be based on past evaluations, on feedback from beneficiaries and from other stakeholders. The procedures for operational planning will also differ from small to large organisations, since the latter are likely to require greater coordination.

SPECIFYING OBJECTIVES AND INDICATORS

Planning a PME process can of course only happen if the organisation's projects, or programmes, and its own progress have themselves been planned for, although a case can sometimes be made for unplanned work too, where creativity, innovation or very rapidly changing circumstances demand it. Two components, that

> **Box 4.4 Specifying Objectives and Indicators**
>
> ✓ Objectives are often overambitious and vaguely formulated. To make them clearer, realistic and more measurable, it is helpful to reflect on the desired final situation, preferably at the start of a project or initiative. The final situation (or dream) should describe what needs changing (quantitatively and qualitatively), specifically for whom (beneficiary group category) and by when. We can stimulate staff and beneficiaries to be as specific as possible. The more detailed the image of the final situation, the easier it is to arrive at concrete indicators. Four questions help to clarify objectives and to link them with indicators:
>
> - What are the objectives of the programme/initiative?
> - What is the desired final situation for the beneficiaries when the organisation can withdraw?
> - What are the key areas of expected success?
> - What are the key indicators of expected success?

follow each other naturally, nevertheless normally stand out as part of the planning process: (*a*) establishing clear, feasible and measurable objectives and (*b*) planning/identifying indicators (see Box 4.4).

'Beneficiaries' are often neglected here: yet when we stimulate their participation as rigorously as possible, we have found their insights about the final desired situation, and ways to measure this, invaluable. Moreover, when an organisation and its beneficiaries both agree on common indicators as satisfying their respective information needs, their interest and commitment in subsequent steps is enhanced.

STRATEGIC PLAN, ON PAPER OR IN HEADS?

Strategic planning is currently receiving much emphasis—often from donors—to encourage organisations to reflect on their strengths and opportunities and choose the best way forward. Unfortunately, many organisations invite consultants to produce such plans for them, while they continue with their routine work, thus divorcing such exercises from actual planning needs and work on the ground. Strategic planning then rarely becomes an institutionalised practice, informed by internal needs and a clear policy. For a more positive outcome, consultants and facilitators should support internal reflection and the development of a strategic plan by the staff themselves. This may take more time, but is often worth the investment.

CONNECTING STRATEGY AND OPERATIONS

Partner organisations have indicated that help to clearly connect strategic and operational planning is especially welcome. Non-governmental organisations often put strategic issues and objectives at one end of their strategic document without incorporating them in their operational plan. The latter then suffers from gaps and lacks detail (including financial detail). The facilitator can help by asking where, in the operational plan, each of the issues/objectives listed in the strategic plan are detailed in terms of *what exactly has to be achieved, how* it is going to be achieved and *at what cost* (see Box 4.5).

Box 4.5 Facilitating Strategic Thinking in an Indian NGO

Bosco Reach Out, an Indian NGO with strong 'grass roots' links, has learnt with the help of a PME facilitator to think strategically, rather than simply producing strategic plans on paper. The NGO constantly scans its internal and external environment, from the perspective of needs, opportunities and capacities. The choice of programmes, strategies and partners keeps evolving, without the NGO loosing control over the situation, or growing haphazardly. Bosco Reach Out thus retains a dynamic character and is not bogged down by the weight of its own decisions.

This is helped by institutionalised PME practices: a PME policy describes the purpose and levels of PME, its process and frequency at each level and the persons to be involved. This policy was developed after five years of systematic PME practice, guided at different stages by a facilitator, once it became clear that the staff had internalised PME concepts and had achieved a degree of consistency in their work. Since then, an organisational evaluation is undertaken every five–six years, followed by a strategic planning exercise. The terms of reference for the evaluations are developed in a participatory workshop attended by various stakeholders. The strategic planning exercises address the important issues identified in the evaluation and by the stakeholders. Decisions are then taken and road maps agreed upon. Periodic reviews take place more frequently and strategic thinking

is an ongoing practice. Projects are planned in keeping with the identified strategic issues and are regularly monitored in accordance with the PME policy. Projects above a certain size are always evaluated by external persons.

This process has been helped by the facilitator's sustained efforts during the strategic planning events and reviews, which were used as opportunities to underline the importance of dynamic strategic thinking. This requires constant monitoring of the external and internal contexts, including changing donor priorities, rather than simply developing a static strategic planning document. Strategy formulation and planning processes were also facilitated with an in-house team nurtured to coordinate them, thus allowing the facilitator to gradually phase out.

THE LOGFRAME: SERVANT OR VILLAIN?

The logframe has been the source of much confusion as a planning tool. Some practitioners are enthusiastic about its use; others quite sceptical. Users often find it helps them to be more logical and focused in planning projects. Logframes can also provide a transparent means of showing what is to be done, against which actions can be measured, so that accountability is improved. And logframes can ease relationships with donors, who are often familiar with such formats.

As facilitators, we must, however, also recognise the problems many users experience with logframes. For a start, they are often found so complicated (including the use of English), that they exclude the very people who should play critical roles in the planning, implementation and M&E of projects. Others see logframes as donor-designed instruments that impose a method of thinking that emphasises predictable change. Day-to-day realities and process issues, unexpected challenges, changes in government policy and so on, can divorce the contents of a logframe from the realities of life on the ground. Third, logframe users may become dependent on them, especially when imposed by donors, thus inhibiting creativity. Fourth, when reports have to be written with reference to a logframe, these tend to be tailored to the project document rather than project experiences. Finally, logframes are more difficult to use where an entire organisation or several overlapping projects or programmes have to be considered simultaneously.

What can facilitators do to make the logframe digestible and useful? Demystifying it by carefully explaining its internal logic can create a positive environment and contribute to learning and self-confidence. We make other suggestions in Box 4.6.

Box 4.6 Domesticating the Logframe

✓ Given the difficulties involved, it is best to only use the logframe in organisations where skills and experiences allow for its effective use, or where these skills can be developed.

✓ As an alternative, and to develop a logical ('narrative') first column, we can visualise this column as a ladder (see Box 2.4) and encourage users to start at the top of the ladder, thus linking the logframe contents to the organisational mission/vision and helping to explore the linkages with programmes. Using a story line, we can also show how one event leads to another, provided the assumptions hold (see also Box 4.13).

✓ A logframe should thus give 'a story', not be used as a way to manipulate terminology. This means helping users focus on the logical thinking process and not just on the final step, that of filling in the boxes of the format. Similarly, the framework should not be used as a stand alone document, without analytical narrative.

✓ We can also clarify that the logframe is both a planning and an M&E tool and not a rigid instrument that cannot be changed after its elaboration. Learning in this context necessitates its regular updating, including the choice of indicators; keeping an open mind for unintended effects or impacts; reviewing the mix of activities, the relevance, specificity and feasibility of objectives; and the validity of the assumptions made.

INSPIRING BUDGETING

Budgeting is often perceived as a dull part of the planning process, especially when it is not used as a management tool, when budgets just live their own lives, used only as cost-controlling devices.

Controlling is, however, not only about checking: it is also about ensuring that higher organisational results, as well as outputs, are achieved. Budgeting must therefore be fully integrated with planning and with M&E at all levels, and used as a task-setting and result-oriented management tool, thus acting as a bridge between planning and M&E. This means moving away from the traditional emphasis on past performance (taking last year's budget, adding inflation and some new cost items), towards budgeting as an integral part of overall plans, to achieve things in the *future*. Budgets then express the objectives of the organisation in financial terms; they form the basis for establishing priorities, allocating resources, measuring performance and ultimately learning to improve. Monitoring and evaluation can then, for instance, show that an objective will only be reached by spending *more* money, or by spending it differently. Discussing how the budget should be *altered*, not to adhere to the agreed limit, becomes important. Budgeting, as an integral part of PME, helps align strategic objectives and focus attention on the future.

Budgets then also become important means of communication, helping to translate plans into tasks and mandates for different people, or departments, in the organisation to contribute to higher common objectives. Budgeting assumes a coordination function; it provides a basis for comparison and corrective action during implementation and for allocating the available funds to different parts of the organisation, reflecting achievement of targets and objectives. Further, by estimating the costs of planned activities (through a transparent cost-allocation system) and delegating authority to spend against these activity costs, the motivation of budget-holders is increased.

Box 4.7 Two Complementary Approaches to Budgeting

Budgeting, as usually understood:

- Resource utilisation—ensuring that resources are utilised for the intended purposes.
- Cost control—creating financial discipline and cost-consciousness.
- Monitoring/evaluation—assessing implementation.

Budgeting can usefully be complemented with:

- Reflecting on the desired future—ensuring result-orientation (accountability for results).
- Motivating the budget-holders—coordinating and communicating management insights and policies.
- Monitoring and evaluation—assessing result-performance and cost-effectiveness for organisational learning.

While small and young organisations may not be able to do so immediately, they could anticipate and decide when the time has come to upgrade their P(Budgeting)ME systems in this direction (see Boxes 4.7 and 4.8).

> **Box 4.8 Effective Plans and Budgets**
>
> ✓ Support by managers often has to be stimulated by involving them in our facilitation process; managers must provide essential information to budget holders if they are to accept accountability for results at higher levels.
>
> ✓ The elaboration of plans and budgets should cultivate the delegation of authority and accountability whenever possible: budgets should be made by the staff or departments that are responsible for their implementation. This will inform who to involve in the facilitation process.
>
> ✓ We need to foster systems where budgets are prepared on a consistent basis, using agreed concepts, procedures and assumptions, linked to a formally established and regular monitoring and review system.
>
> ✓ This will enhance ownership and motivation and can then be managed through a flexible and informative accounting system to compare actual progress against plan and budget.

ISSUES IN M&E: DATA COLLECTION

Facilitating the development, or review, of a monitoring framework involves a number of issues, such as the type of data required, how it will be collected and analysed, how often and by whom. We focus here on a few aspects that, in our experience, often require support.

DROWNING IN DATA

Any M&E system must generate information needed for decision-making. Yet, we often find an overkill of information, hindering utility and blocking decisions. This frequently happens with output- and activity-oriented M&E and worsens once effect and impact monitoring is added to the workload, which then acts as a disincentive to increase the scope of M&E to these levels. Service delivery organisations, especially those dealing with large volumes of regular data (credit recovery rate, percentage of immunised children and the like) may also miss out on crucial aspects of performance. In a savings and credit programme we worked on, for example, the profitability of the credit cooperatives, an important indicator for programme success, was not being monitored for this reason.

External requirements, be it by donors (especially multiple ones, with various demands), or by governments, can also lead to information overload. As we saw earlier, the scope of a PME system (including the balance between improving and proving) affects the volume of data produced. Internal mechanisms may be at fault too, as in organisations where leaders insist on controlling staff by collecting detailed information, thus undermining organisation-wide learning, which requires delegation and participation. As facilitators, we can help improve information management so that it really contributes to learning and sound decision-making, for example, by evaluating minimum information needs (see Box 4.9).

The methods and tools used and the frequency of data collection can also be rationalised. We often see high expectations of tools, magically lifting practitioners from PME misery, offering a shortcut for hard work and effortlessly generating useful information. If new tools proliferate, what seems to persist, however, is their inappropriate application. Tools and methods must match users' capacities. This is especially so where compilation is concerned: how the data will be compiled must be visualised upfront, to avoid unused information. Overload can also turn the implementing organisation into a monitoring one: we need to be alert to such risk, especially where organisations are over-ambitious when planning their data collection, oblivious of the implications on resources and ultimately on implementation capacity. Elaborate studies with many open-ended questions and participatory appraisal exercises can be especially burdensome. While a large organisation with dedicated task forces may opt for large surveys, a mid-size one will prefer to carry out assessments on a sample basis at larger intervals and to involve those collecting information in its compilation as well.

Box 4.9 Avoiding Information Overload

✓ In addition to clarifying information flows (see Box 4.11), much can be gained from simplicity. There is no need to measure the obvious or the already known, and it is better to be approximately right than precisely wrong.

✓ There is no point in collecting information if it is not compiled and analysed and we can often help reduce indicator numbers, sample sizes and frequencies of measurement. Measuring the effects and impacts of routine projects is, for instance, less important (even superfluous) than of those with an experimental character.

✓ It is useful to start by discussing the 'real' information needs of the organisation, independent of external needs. What is needed, for instance, to help management learn and make efficient decisions? How do these information needs compare with external needs?

✓ By clarifying the scope of PME, we can also encourage a focus on results and the total organisation, away from a sole concern with activities.

✓ An analysis of the current information system, both formal and informal, provides a good starting point for any additions, improvements and simplifications. We can then help develop a flexible, step-by-step system. Indicators can be added, or deleted, or the monitoring of the quality of activities, or results may begin once the organisation is comfortable with managing quantitative data, with the latter only gathered at large intervals. The perspective and expertise of staff to assess quality often needs to be strengthened as part of this process.

Beyond Activities

We often see a PME focus on activities, rather than on desired long-term changes. This often arises when information about activities is easier to gather than about effects and impacts. In many contexts, accomplishing activities can also, in itself, be satisfying, even exhilarating. Formal PME practice then acquires a narrow data collection focus: on field activities, for instance, with little linkage to other sources of information in the organisation and the external context. Yet, development organisations are in existence to accomplish more than activities. They will themselves mention the changes they, their beneficiaries and donors want to see as a result of their activities, or programmes, and that justify their existence as an organisation. Engulfed in day-to-day challenges, they need reminding of these 'higher level' considerations. And, rather than shying away from impact assessment and efficient use of resources, they need help to focus on these, using tools and approaches that are commensurate with their skills, ambitions and contexts (see Box 4.10).

Our experience also reminds us that every organisation is unique: if results are always relevant, in smaller organisations with limited staff, for example, data collection may have to be selectively planned to indicate success, or failure. A new organisation may

Box 4.10 Choosing Tools to Go Beyond Activities

A wide variety of tools and techniques are available to go beyond activities, including PRA-related tools, videos, story telling, popular theatre, quantitative tools such as community surveys, and tools derived from the anthropological tradition, such as participant observation and oral testimonies. These can also be used for planning, analysis and reporting. While a choice of tools—including those that visualise change, such as drawings, pictograms, charts and the like—will depend on context and type of organisation, other questions can also be posed:

- Where can the information be found?
- Who will have the professional experience to deal with particular tools?
- Who will therefore gather the information?
- When and how frequently will the information be collected?

only gradually venture into qualitative data collection and a small one may avoid it altogether as the relevant discussions will in any case take place. In larger, older organisations, which may have specialised monitoring staff, the quality of activities may be measured on a sample basis. Still, a large organisation with a dedicated team for M&E will only need to collect impact-level data periodically, although it will examine specific issues using more in-depth research methods (see Box 4.11).

Box 4.11 Information Flows

✓ We have found it useful to help partner organisations distinguish between information flows related to (a) activities and outputs and (b) effects and impacts, and to discuss their consequences for information management. Generally, compiling information, analysing it and making decisions is desirable at the 'lowest' possible organisational level:

- Information related to *activities* and *outputs* is normally generated during project implementation and is important for field staff to keep on track and ensure quality delivery. It does not all need to be channelled to the rest of the organisation and can be aggregated as it travels, as only a few selected output indicators are likely to be important for, say, the organisation's management, that might only need information on the rate of execution of the work plan and how the budget is spent. Unless serious problems arise, or an activity is experimental, the more routine the activities, the fewer the indicators needed at 'higher' levels.

- Information related to *effects* and *impacts* is generated using only key indicators. At the lowest level, such indicators produce information and knowledge (possibly leading to some decisions), which is then used by the rest of the organisation, where each level adds its own information and enriches the analysis for the same indicators. Aggregation then takes place for analysis and, ideally, participatory decision-making.

MEASURING QUALITATIVE CHANGE

If organisations can often track change in terms of quantity, quality aspects can be more challenging. Even when an organisation is engaged in clear-cut service delivery, a quality dimension is often sought, such as beneficiary participation in the service provided (see Box 4.12).

Several problems can arise. Qualitative information can be biased when an organisation believes positive information will

Box 4.12 Quantifying Quality: The Case of a Network in Mali

The network 'Réseau Plaidoyer et Lobby' supports its NGO members country-wide. Over the years, the distribution of tasks had become vague, with the secretariat at times taking over responsibilities from members, or members expecting services from the secretariat that were not in keeping with its original mandate.

While facilitating the network to explore this issue, one of the indicators for improved performance was the 'number of members' requests sent to central office'. This proved of limited use, as this number would in itself be of little importance. Instead, 'the nature of the requests sent by the members' proved a more powerful effect indicator as to how the members had understood the role of the central office. How could this be quantified as well?

This could be facilitated by splitting the issue into more manageable dimensions, categorising the requests, some of which could be classified as fitting with the newly agreed mandate, while others would fall outside it. Counting the requests in each category over the years could thus be used to track members' perceptions of the central office and how this evolved. The success of the capacity-building activities and of the growth in members' competences could also be derived from the table, thus presenting a simple combination of quantity and quality.

Type of requests	2005	2006	2007
Formulation of indicators			
Understanding of basic terminology			
Project proposal development			
Data analysis			
Finance			
Others			

elicit continued donor support, such as when a single case study is presented as evidence of a result. More often, qualitative indicators prove challenging. They are often said to be necessary to illustrate a process taking place: is this so and how can we tackle this as facilitators? One way is to help partner organisations think about the story behind a quantitative indicator, looking for deeper meaning. For example, 'level of income', as a result of micro-enterprise development, can be described as a 'hard' economic indicator, and yet, if we measure increased incomes over a sustained period, what does it tell us? We can first verify who benefited. Was it the particular group we had in mind? This could tell us whether we have progressed in achieving our vision/mission. We can then ask which factors contributed to this increased income. The answers (best found by talking to those directly involved) may include: 'we now speak to people we never spoke to before', or 'we feel more independent, the relations with our husbands have changed'. Such answers will be more emphatic if incomes are increased over a period: looking at the time dimension then becomes a practical way to address the indicator of sustainability.

This example shows how to select indicators of social, or attitudinal, change, by thinking carefully about what one expects people to do, for instance, when becoming more independent, and by breaking expected change into manageable, identifiable components. Thus, convincing bank officials to approve a larger loan for a business could be an indication of greater confidence. Turning this into an indicator 'number and types of loans accessed by group x of women entrepreneurs' then becomes both a quantitative and qualitative indicator, combining economic and social dimensions. Similarly, women being elected on local councils might indicate growing independence. This can be rephrased as 'number of women elected in representative bodies in y position'. Such an approach opens new ways of developing indicators and can shortcut endless discussions on process indicators.

AWAY FROM INDICATORS?

Where indicators are found to be too rigid to describe complex changes, or where alternatives better in tune with oral cultures

Box 4.13 Using the 'Significant Change' Method

Stories people tell about changes offer a striking characteristic: three types of change often surface, whether at the personal or collective level: (a) a change in living conditions in a broad sense, (b) a change in capacity to organise and (c) a policy change. A savings and credit group in Rwanda described its success thus:

Type of change	Living conditions	Organisation capacity	Policy
Individual	Higher savings, incomes and ability to purchase new assets.	Ability to manage larger loans and organise new activities.	More equal relation with husband; more outgoing; elected on representative bodies.
Group	Increased saving volume and more loans accessed.	High performance as a group; high repayment rates; access to bank loans.	Able to convince bank of credit-worthiness and able to change banking policy accordingly.

This resembles the three intervention strategies to alleviate structural poverty that donors often refer to: (a) direct poverty alleviation, (b) society building and organisational capacity and (c) policy change. This similarity gives the facilitator an opportunity to link perspectives on changes, which stakeholders might initially understand differently. It helps to build a common understanding of different result levels (effects and impacts) and their indicators. Such linking can also improve the quality of communication between donor and partner organisation.

are sought, the 'significant change' method (see Further Reading) provides an alternative. We have, for instance, found community groups responding to questions about what has significantly changed in their environment in a detailed and precise manner (which in turn yields perceptive and measurable indicators). This can be done with specific sub-groups in a community and facilitating this jointly with partner organisation staff has an important added value: by demonstrating the capacity of such groups to clearly describe their experiences of changes, such unexpectedly rich information may alter staff perception of their 'target' population. The method can also stimulate creative thinking: we have, for instance, found unexpected 'significant changes' described by beneficiaries forcing NGO staff to question the assumptions that informed the design of their programme.

Story telling offers a similar alternative. Staff can, for instance, be invited to tell stories of real successes, or painful failures, and will often do so without restraint. Such stories can then be discussed to yield patterns. When a story is used to illustrate changes, this is often dismissed as anecdotal evidence and rarely considered as 'proof' by outsiders. While a single story may indeed be anecdotal, a great number of them, told by different people in different places, may be cross-checked and assessed for consistency. In a development organisation, field staff may be invited to collect such stories and these can be used to stimulate organisation-wide learning (see Box 4.13).

NEVER TOO LATE FOR A BASELINE!

To answer questions such as 'How much have we progressed since the start of our intervention? Why? Why not?', a conventional baseline is established at the start of a project, usually with a large data set, often covering wide-ranging socio-economic information on a population. It may be updated 10 years later, if at all. Baselines tend to be static, rarely looked at again during implementation and seldom used for M&E purposes. Donors may be asking for a baseline, but hardly ever indicate its desired scope and how it may be used for M&E. A baseline is then of little value as a management tool; it is an expensive exercise and can cover up a lack of project focus too.

How then can we help partners develop a baseline that provides a useful point of reference? Where programme focus is clear and where outcome and impact indicators have been selected, these can be used for a baseline. The current values of these indicators (irrespective of whether an initiative is just starting or partly implemented), can present the baseline. It can be used from that moment onwards and can consist of only the key effect and impact indicators, as the most important yardsticks to measure progress. Being part of a regular M&E system, this baseline will be updated every time effect and/or impact monitoring takes place. Just as indicators may change over time, the baseline also adapts, using new indicators and perhaps dropping old ones. The baseline then acquires a dynamic, rolling character and becomes a relevant internal management tool. Further, it should step over artificial programme borders, take a long-term perspective and act as an illustration of the organisation's mission/vision; no longer a large collection of socio-demographic data, but much more focused on the role of the organisation. Even where it does not take place at the outset of a development initiative, a baseline can, in our experience, be extremely stimulating: it gives the staff a fresh look at a situation and even forces them to question their approach and propose corrections. Finally, as the example in Box 4.14 shows, a baseline need not be a large-scale undertaking: small is possible and can combine practicality with usefulness.

Box 4.14 Small is Beautiful: A Promising Baseline in Malawi

In a Malawi paprika-growing project involving contract farming between farmers and a processing and trading company, a baseline provides an initial point of reference. It helps to establish whether contract farming is a win-win situation for both parties and why. The baseline set the initial values for a set of indicators, focusing on a few elements (farmers' current income sources, market developments, pricing of inputs, contract appreciation, etc.).

Over the next few years, these indicators will be measured annually in the slack season to inform on progress, obstacles, unintended effects and thus lead to changes in activities and approaches, as well as with regard to M&E: choice of indicators, other data collection methodology, sample size, etc.

Contract farmers exceed 1,000. The sample size is 45 farmers, distributed over the production area; representatives of the company; the paprika associations and community leaders. Though small, the sample provides very valuable information, both quantitative and qualitative.

Control Groups: Ethical, Useful, Realistic?

Linked to baselines, is the use of control groups. When collecting information on effects and impacts for a beneficiary group, an important (but often overlooked) issue is whether to look beyond this group to, say, a nearby community. Observing similar changes in both groups can be interpreted as evidence that an initiative was not effective, since it yielded no change. This view can, however, be short-sighted: wishing to see the success of our activity spread to other groups, we may seek a multiplier effect. Observing similar changes in the control group can then strengthen a claim of success. Using a control group to arrive at a judgement of changes in people's lives is thus often necessary, although establishing any cause–effect relation is a challenge which also raises ethical and cost issues. At times though, the use of control groups can result in a greater impact than many small-scale programmes can otherwise have (see Box 4.15). Randomised evaluations are also feasible: they are labour-intensive and costly, but often no more so than other data-collection

Box 4.15 Exploiting Non-beneficiaries? Using Control Groups

The International Christian Support Fund in Kenya (ICSK) runs a health programme in Kenyan primary schools, which, from its start, has been accompanied by a large data collection exercise. This exercise, using randomised evaluation, is extensive compared to the health programme itself; it entails splitting schools into two categories (one group receives the intervention while the other—the control group—does not). The effect of the intervention is determined by subsequently assessing differences between the groups.

The reactions from the schools, the project staff and donor representatives to this form of evaluation ranged from disbelief to demands to abandon such an 'unethical method' (deliberately leaving out a needy population from the project and spending much money on data collection). By adopting this methodology, ICSK has, however, been able to prove (in an objective way) that their approach really works. This helps them to market the project to others, who now implement it on a larger scale. The national government and World Bank officials have been convinced of the value of this type of health intervention and are planning to replicate it nationwide.

procedures. They can be conducted over time and, once staff are trained, they can work for several projects: since data collection is the most costly element of these evaluations, 'cross-cutting' a sample significantly reduces costs.

ARE ALL BENEFICIARIES THE SAME?

Partner organisations often describe their beneficiary group as homogeneous: 'They are all poor and marginalised.' Yet we know that development processes are not neutral: some people benefit more and some may lose out. Many organisations we have worked with have made a start in recognising differences with regard to gender, but rarely go further (such as differences in age, wealth, education, religion, or ethnicity). Categories may overlap: people may simultaneously hold a mix of identities and some may change (education, economic occupation). Other attributes, such as access to power, resources, and regulatory frameworks, may also be crucial in influencing how effects and impacts are appropriated by people. All this calls for PME practice that recognises differences and thus improves performance. The 'social relations approach' developed

Box 4.16 Facilitating a Disaggregated Approach to 'Beneficiary' Groups

We have found Naila Kabeer's five sets of questions useful to help 'unpack' beneficiary groups:

Rules	How do things get done? Who is favoured by these rules? Who is not?
Members	Who is in? Who is out? Who belong to this institution? Who does not?
Activities	What is done? By whom?
Resources	What resources are being used and produced?
Power	Who decides and whose interests are served? Who can change the rules?

by Naila Kabeer is useful to describe institutions (marriage, communities, markets, etc. See 'Further Reading'). This model can be used everywhere and creates lively debates (see Box 4.16). It helps make people aware of changes in institutions as a result of interventions and to ask which indicators best capture such changes for purposes of M&E.

WHO IS INVOLVED?

Another issue concerns who will collect data, how and how often. Here again we need to keep in mind the different levels at which an organisation functions, the hierarchy of results that it seeks to achieve and the corresponding, but varied information sources: information on budgets and costs, on progress of activities, on effects and impacts, on the wider context and the like.

Different information sources imply the participation of various stakeholders in their collection (and analysis, as we see next). Field staff and communities can often easily gather information on outputs and project progress. They may also collect data on effects and impacts although this may require external assistance. We have seen organisations, particularly mid-size ones, ask their field staff to gather qualitative data. Usually better equipped to implement activities, they can find collecting this in an open-ended and objective manner difficult, with a tendency to prove rather than measure, setting in. To measure qualitative information through recording anecdotal evidence, quotes and the like requires special skills. A decision then has to be made on whether building these skills is the best investment, or whether other resource persons are needed.

ISSUES IN M&E: ANALYSIS AND DECISION-MAKING

THE CHALLENGE OF ANALYSIS

Before any data can be analysed, systematic collation (which determines the quality and ease of subsequent analysis) needs

Organisations can be exploitative when they are not able to plan their M&E, do not assign a budget to it, or state that the information is important to the 'beneficiary', whereas it only serves their own information needs. Beneficiaries are then used as providers of cheap labour to gather data (often under the guise of 'participation').

There can, however, be a symbiosis of information needs, where data collection is physically shared without payment and without the population feeling used. Thus, when an Indian NGO started to actively monitor water levels in wells (initially for their own purpose), community members realised the importance of this information, as it underlined the seriousness of the water situation in their area. This stimulated them to ban drilling further wells and to request the NGO to continue monitoring this indicator. Although the NGO no longer needed this information, it joined the community and facilitated well monitoring. Shared data collection and analysis can be a powerful stimulus for action.

attention from facilitators: staff often need effective formats to stimulate careful data collection and trigger analysis. We often find that information gathered is rarely analysed, fed back to the 'grass-roots' and regularly used for decision-making. This adds to a perception of reporting as a burden with no visible benefit, especially among busy field staff.

A culture of lack of analysis and critical review is then allowed to prevail. When asked 'Who does the analysis?', staff often respond 'higher management'. If asked to reflect on participation and organisational learning, however, they will quickly agree that analysis must involve stakeholders at different levels in an organisation. Analysis is indeed about engaging participants in critical reflection on the results and causes of organisational efforts– some of which they are directly responsible for. For most field staff this is a logical observation, as they often have been doing precisely that with beneficiaries, albeit informally. In some cases too, such reflection may require collecting further monitoring information over the next operational period.

Data collection and analysis should therefore be connected wherever possible. Field staff involved in data collection will, for instance, also want to add their views and interpretations and, given their close relation to any beneficiary group, are often in the best position to suggest changes and report any unforeseen effects. Ignoring such contributions undermines ownership and participation in PME processes. In smaller and younger organisations, facilitators may wish to encourage the participation of *all* staff when analysing data. It is also possible to help programme and finance personnel work together and see the relation between progress in both areas. Beneficiaries should also participate: in collaboration with field staff, their analysis and interpretation of field data can prove immensely useful (see Box 4.17).

Taking and Sharing Decisions and Learning from Them

No M&E is useful if it does not result in decision-making for the next operating period. Decisions can be as complex as changing strategies, or as simple as deciding that information is insufficient to make a sound decision. They may also be taken at different levels: field staff may take decisions, following their shared analysis with the beneficiary group on the effect of an activity. Sometimes intervention decisions may be taken solely within an organisation; at others, various stakeholders are involved, with differing needs and interests.

We have often experienced poor quality in decision-making: decisions are taken, but not well implemented; management shies away from difficult ones; too much personal power or interest is at play. It is also common to hear staff in larger organisations, or members in networks, complain of ignorance of decisions made by management, or the executive committee. Once information travels upwards in an organisation, a perception often develops that the responsibility for monitoring and bringing change rests exclusively with 'experts' and senior colleagues, and efforts towards finding locally appropriate solutions reduce, with field or 'junior' staff being excluded, thus removing their opportunity to contribute critical views to decisions (see Box 4.18).

An effective decision-making system is necessary, yet PME facilitators often stop at the data collection and compilation stages,

Box 4.18 Involvement in Analysis is Energising

Planning, monitoring and evaluation facilitators engaged the new director of Purvanchal Gramin Chetna, a 25-year-old Indian NGO, in a dialogue about making the planning and monitoring process more transparent and participatory. Soon, the staff at the lower levels experienced a refreshing change.

Guided by the facilitators, the director began by involving the staff in the planning of a new project. The results expected from them and the approach to follow were clarified. Next, the facilitators designed a monitoring system with them, guiding them to collect data and to analyse it at their own level. The system has worked well and the sense of purpose and motivation much improved.

Analysis, however, did not come easily: objectivity was a major challenge, given an initial tendency to justify areas of limited accomplishment and to blame the context or the community. Thanks to assurances by the facilitators and the director that no one would be victimised, critical discussions began on reasons for successes and failures, and learning drawn from them. Best practices have steadily emerged since.

The regional offices of Purvanchal Gramin Chetna display results, including social issues taken up by partner community groups and the manner in which local governments are challenged to provide quality services. A matrix is available in all offices, with photographs and data on such successes. The staff are clear on their level of success, on any shortcomings and openly seek possible alternatives.

when they should ensure the development of a complete system, including a decision-making and communication strategy. In mid-size organisations, for instance, as the numbers of staff, projects and departments increase, it is important to decide who continues to be involved in data analysis and in decision-making meetings. Not everyone must always be present, but some inter-linkages must exist and meetings must take place periodically to ensure synergy and coordination. In larger organisations, facilitators can help ensure that each level assesses its own performance according to their analysis of information and takes decisions that are within its powers. For the rest, we can suggest what must be considered for decision-making at the next level. The decision-making powers at each level must be clearly defined, and will depend on the organisation' attitude to experimenting and to delegating such powers. In networks, participation by all member organisations is essential: even where decisions are made by an elected executive committee, these should be communicated to maintain transparency and interest across the network.

FEEDBACK AND MONITORING THE IMPLEMENTATION OF DECISIONS

Feedback is needed to close the PME cycle. Decisions have consequences, positive or not, for all in the organisation. Sound feedback to those concerned is therefore crucial. Without it, those who have been involved in the previous steps and contributed to the decisions, will quickly loose interest in their role in PME.

Feedback needs to follow clear rules—whether written or not—as to how information is used and disseminated to reach those concerned. We find that this remains a neglected area in some organisations, especially where they are grappling with data collection, at the expense of analysis, documentation and decision-making. PME facilitators can help ensure feedback by not leaving the support process once a PME system has been designed or reviewed. They can time their availability and involvement to help assess whether the organisation has the mechanisms to recall decisions taken at the end of the previous cycle and whether the implementation of decisions is monitored.

Finally, facilitators need to create space to periodically review with their partners the monitoring system itself, with a view to improvements, especially in its initial stages. It cannot be assumed that organisations will have a complete and optimal M&E system in place from the outset. Yet, without it, it is difficult to say something pertinent about *why* the results that are noted at target group level were or were not achieved, let alone *what* interventions are needed to improve results. An organisation will therefore first have to learn how to improve its monitoring system before learning how to improve results, just like an organisation that has begun with evaluations will first learn how to improve its planning. Improving monitoring systems, as a result of a frank evaluation, may, for example, lead to adding, removing, or altering indicators, so that

Box 4.19 Reflecting on an M&E System

✓ We have found that the following questions can stimulate reflection on M&E system and practice:

- How much data is being collected? Is it sufficient or excessive, affecting implementation? Is the data being correctly collected? Are the formats used for M&E clear and consistent?
- Can the results be reasonably attributed to the intervention? Is information sufficient to come to this conclusion? Is additional information needed and what indicators may provide this?
- Is all analysed information useful to learn about these results, is some superfluous? Is it being analysed at the appropriate organisational level? Is management looking into critical indicators of success or getting lost in details?
- Are consultations and reflection with all stakeholders sufficient? Is it leading to institutional learning and is this learning documented? What learning opportunities are available to enhance organisational M&E skills and do they clash with implementation demands?
- Are clear decisions made at various levels, not made, or made only in a centralised manner? Are these decisions communicated both 'upwards' and 'downwards' as and when required?

the evaluative questions can be better answered and informed decisions taken (see Box 4.19).

Such support is essential in a rapidly growing mid-size organisation. While larger ones may have in-house expertise, or the resources to call in technical support, the leaders of growing organisations should begin to have management information that allows them to gauge progress in the quality of their PME processes.

TIMING: PME CALENDARS

Steps in the PME cycle can be organised and timed over the year. We have found that presenting this cycle in the form of a calendar helps to integrate it into the regular work plan and budget of the organisation. Two different but interrelated processes can be plotted: (a) indicator timing, focusing on the data collection step (timing and frequency of measurement of indicators, especially at the effect and impact levels) (see Box 4.20) and (b) PME scheduling, showing all the PME events taking place in the organisation (analysing data, taking decisions, re-planning, working out new strategic directions and the like) (see Box 4.21).

The first process is mentioned as separate, as it is new and time-consuming for organisations that are less accustomed to monitoring effect and impact, beyond outputs and activities. This process links to the second: the indicator calendar must fit with the total range of annual PME events. Although various planning and budgeting events are an integral part of the work plan, M&E events are often neglected. Yet, when we endeavour to foster learning, attention needs to be paid to planning M&E events in the same way as for other planning sessions. These may be separate events, part of wider planning, or staff meetings. Another calendar can then indicate when regular M&E will take place, who will take part and incorporate PME events for organisation-wide learning as well. Staff can take note of these for their personal plans.

ORGANISATIONAL STRUCTURES FOR PME

In many organisations, planning mechanisms have been developed and sometimes perfected, with clearly defined roles and

Box 4.20 Calendar for Data Collection (of Effects and Impacts): An Example from Accion Fraterna, India

Having established effect and impact indicators, Accion Fraterna (AF) and the facilitators jointly elaborated a calendar for the relevant data collection and the first stage of analysis with the target group. This showed the distribution of the M&E workload through the year, which could be compared with the major field season. Soil conservation and water harvesting works (March–July) demanded much work: M&E was thus shifted, as much as possible, to the slack season (except where M&E indicators were season-bound). Hence, a second version of the calendar, shown here, which provided AF with a good overview of M&E activities and the necessary input to integrate M&E within the overall work plan.

General objective	Impact indicators	Jan	Feb	Mar	Apr	May	Jun	Jul	Aug	Sept	Oct	Nov	Dec
Improved livelihood	Purchase of assets	x	x										
Specific objectives	Effect indicators												
1. Dry land, water and forest management	Quality of maintenance of soil and water conservation structures		x										
	Area under traditional paddy								x	x			
	Type, extent of water saving practices								x	x			
	Survival rate of seedlings planted						x						
2. Linking with government	Volume of government support to watershed programmes (Rupees)			x		x							
	Survival rate of seedlings planted						x						

Developing such a calendar for data collection (first as a stand alone exercise and later comparing it with workloads for project implementation) is a useful facilitators' step to illustrate the linkage between a so-called M&E plan and the overall work plan. M&E then becomes part and parcel of the work plan.

Box 4.21 An Overall Planning, Budgeting and M&E Calendar

When facilitating an overall calendar to implement planning, budgeting, monitoring and evaluation (PBME) for a Philippino NGO, as shown here, we learnt that such a calendar should reflect a PBME cycle that continues from year to year, in the same way that a strategic plan should be reviewed on the basis of annual performance and other M&E information. We also learnt that M&E events need special attention, while planning and budgeting events are more easily mentioned. In view of these, the NGO decided that their organisational learning would only take place when all personnel, including field, accounting and other support staff, attend PME meetings as an interdisciplinary group.

(a) Planning Cycle (Including Budgeting)		
January–May	Strategic plan review: performance evaluation of previous year and update; scanning of environment and internal organisation (discuss/update strategic objectives).	
June–September	Implementation plan for total organisation (strategies, projects and programmes). Target-group plans, organisational development plans, including financial plan, human resource plan, indicators and M&E plan.	
October–December	Operational planning and budgeting. Departments, projects and programmes (adding up to total organisation).	
(b) Monitoring and Evaluation/Assessment Cycle		
Monthly, quarterly and half-yearly meetings for monitoring, reporting, evaluation and decision-making	Monitoring schedule.	Plan of tasks to gather monitoring data (by whom and when—monthly/quarterly/yearly).
	Reporting schedule and contents of reports.	What reports to be issued when and at what level.
	Evaluation/assessment schedules.	Attended by all management and staff; beneficiary group and stakeholders participation.
	Decision-making meetings	Resulting decisions for the plans/budgets agreed and documented (beginning of following month/quarter/etc.)

responsibilities. When it comes to M&E, however, and especially effect and impact monitoring, such roles and responsibilities often need to be clarified. This can start with assigning roles and responsibilities to all involved in PME, a crucial element for participation and thus ownership. We have found that two issues recur:

THE ROLE OF A PME UNIT

Large organisations often have a specialised PME unit. We often see that, when initially building up expertise, such a unit can play a useful role in supporting overall PME in the organisation, as long as it refrains from implementation (see Box 4.22). One must indeed be sensitive to the risk of alienating PME for other staff, leading to a perception that unit personnel are there to check on others. In

Box 4.22 The PME Unit—An Informal Resource at the Association of Church Development Projects, Ghana

The Association of Church Development Projects (ACDEP) gathers 40 ecumenical organisations in its network, training members and, more recently, strengthening their PME capacity.

To do so, because of its own limitations, the secretariat set up an M&E resource group, informally attached to ACDEP. This mostly consists of PME professionals (with varied levels of experience), each employed in different organisations, but willing to help ACDEP members improve PME practices and systems. The group also includes a few managers of ACDEP member organisations, ready to share their know-how.

While the informality of this group can complicate planning (contributions are voluntary), the skills of the PME professionals match the different sectors ACDEP members are engaged in. Moreover, ACDEP has assessed its members' PME capacity, which helps to identify those resource persons best qualified to help. Members have readily accepted this support group, in part because it is external to them and thus allows them to retain ownership of their own PME systems.

At the request of the ACDEP secretariat, external PME facilitators have helped to build the capacity of the resource group, both to develop a shared vision on PME and in certain topical areas. The personal and informal character of the group strengthens eagerness to absorb new knowledge and experiences from elsewhere. Matching the capacity of each PME professional with the member's focus area and its current PME competence are crucial conditions for success.

some large NGOs in Bangladesh, for instance, PME units effectively control quality, but this is seen as policing and field staff play a rather passive role in M&E. This becomes a challenge for the facilitator, as it may be difficult to question ingrained work methods. It is then important to assess the role, perception and potential of such a unit. Could it contribute to wider learning processes, for instance, by facilitating in-depth research on specific topics and impact?

THE ROLE OF A FINANCE DEPARTMENT

With finance usually seen as a support function in an organisation, this can lead to marginalisation. This is when a finance department operates as a separate island, with staff invisibly busy with bookkeeping, producing annual accounts, reporting to government, or handling taxation matters. As facilitators, we can help change this vision and promote teamwork between finance and programme staff so that 'finance' relates to the overall strategic needs of the organisation and offers its skills to meet the needs of other departments (see Box 4.23). We return to this in the next chapter.

We have, of course, come across other weaknesses, mostly linked to governance issues, such as directors telling an accountant how to post expense claims, board members who know little about finance and leave everything to a so-called 'treasurer', or finance functions that suffer (qualitatively and quantitatively) from understaffing. Increased attention then has to be given to finance and human resources, in terms of numbers, skills, remuneration and decision-making. We may also help with governance: while the accountant, or finance manager, will normally report to the director, given his/her role as the financial conscience of the organisation, s/he may need special authority delegated by the board to exercise certain controls over the director. It is also the responsibility of the board to ensure that sufficient financial checks and balances exist, clearly expressed in the financial policies, and often delegated to the treasurer. In a small organisation, a connection between the bookkeeper and the treasurer is also important, to ensure the integrity of the financial information used in PME.

Box 4.23 Facilitating a More Positive Role for the Finance Department

✓ A good starting point is often to discuss how financial reporting can reflect internal management needs rather than donor requirements and become part of narrative reporting.

✓ It is often necessary to point out that the finance function requires staff that have the skills to relate to the strategic needs of the organisation. This can be helped if finance staff work with programme staff and offer their skills to meet the financial management information needs of other departments. This demands active communication and other skills, beyond those of the 'classical bookkeepers' in the accounts section.

✓ We can show how budgets should be task-setting and reflect the cost of the strategic activities that have been identified as necessary to achieve success. Hence the need to raise 'basic cost accounting' of salaries, office expenditure and the like to 'activity accounting': a person responsible for an activity (or even an entire programme) that he/she believes in, will be interested in making this activity as cost-efficient and cost-effective as possible.

✓ Good working communications between the accountant or financial manager, the treasurer and other board members are essential: this may require facilitation sessions with the individuals concerned.

RESOURCING A PME CYCLE

Information on the specific resources needed to build a PME process and to sustain it as a permanent feature of an organisation's operations is generally lacking. We can nevertheless suggest the following:

FINANCIAL RESOURCES

The availability of financial resources will greatly affect the way PME is conducted. Costs mainly relate to the salaries of staff collecting information and participating in other PME events. Will an organisation accept to incur such costs? The more advanced will recognise that the costs of operating PME systems are intended to avoid waste and to promote organisational learning. To generate sufficient resources for PME, a culture that recognises both PME and learning as essential is important: PME is not a special job to be done (as part of a temporary organisational development project, for example). PME and learning must be seen as critical for success and therefore all 'clients' of the organisation, including donors, should pay their fair share for it (see Box 4.24).

Box 4.24 Resourcing PME

✓ PME saves resources! It helps to differentiate between investment and running costs and to clarify the scope of PME. This is essential, both internally and externally for effective communication with donors.

✓ Where an organisation wants to develop its PME expertise, we can suggest a temporary reduction in activities to create space for PME capacity-building. We find that donors are often willing to support this approach.

✓ It is often valuable to clarify that PME, including informal PME, is part of a daily routine. Plans and budgets should specify PME activities and allocate resources in terms of time, transport, finance, etc.

✓ We can usefully emphasise the need for flexible planning and resource allocation: once PME becomes an integral element of staff tasks, PME will also entail regular reviews of work plans, objectives and strategies, implying that changes will occur from time to time. Effect and impact M&E may also occasionally bring unexpected results, requiring reviews and re-planning, possibly on a regular, maybe annual, basis.

✓ There are very few donors who do not get annoyed by claims that PME costs a lot of money, without a solid explanation of what is actually meant. Helping organisations to communicate effectively with donors is therefore an important facilitation task. Donor and other supporters' education (accepting PME costs in budgets as a structural dimension of development and as productive project costs rather than as overheads) is also vital.

✓ Given the limited documentation on the resources needed to build and sustain PME processes, a good argument exists for facilitators to systematically document their experiences.

When organisations lack clarity about the scope of their PME systems, however, donors might be hesitant to extend support, fearing a costly information collection system. Organisations also often fail to explain that their staff spend much time on M&E informally and that some practices can be formalised, without additional costs. Appropriate effect and impact monitoring, as well as sustaining PME as a learning management tool may, however, require additional skills and resources for staff training and/or hiring additional personnel. Costs might also include staff participation in strategic planning and regular M&E meetings, a key approach to achieving individual and collective organisational learning, as well as to improve internal accountability.

COMPUTERS: THE PME MAGIC BULLET?

PME practice partly depends on familiarity with information technology and systems, as this can enhance the sophistication of information management required for more effective monitoring. However, just as development workers often display a belief in PME tools as a source of salvation, they often express the same with regard to computers, another magic bullet. Larger NGOs may have well established PME systems and make good use of computers for data processing and storing, especially where field stations have access to their own computer-based data instead of relying on a central office (see Box 4.25). While using computers for data analysis can pose challenges, it is especially useful for organisations that implement service-oriented programmes, using standardised indicators. In many cases, off-the-shelf computer packages for data collection and analysis (such as Microsoft Excel) will be adequate, at less cost and difficulty than any custom-made software.

Computers, however, cannot replace personal observation and judgement, establishing reasons behind changes and examining intended and unintended or contextual factors. However efficient a computer is at handling certain types of data and creating some order or aggregation, the final judgement will have to remain in the hands of the staff. In many situations too, computer use is restricted by lack of electricity, finance, or skills. Notebooks, or flipcharts, are

Box 4.25 Pradan's Computer *Munshi*

Pradan works with 100,000 families in several regions of India to promote livelihoods for the rural poor, with a focus on micro-finance.

When Pradan developed its internal learning system (ILS), it had also started to computerise its financial transactions with its 6,000 partner groups. The computer software is run by trained local youth as entrepreneurs, with the ILS data tagged on to these 'computer *munshi* (accountants)'. Information from group diaries (or workbooks, in part pictorial in nature) as filled by their members, is entered into the computer with various qualitative indicators related to group health. This information is merged with the computerised financial indicators and a composite health status report is generated. Simultaneously, the staff supporting each group provide their appreciation, which is also entered. This information is collated and various reports are generated at the group and group cluster levels. In the process, members reflect on their progress through individual and group diaries and get feedback from the staff. The staff are informed on progress made in each group and cluster and identify areas for future interventions. For an impact study, the review of diaries over the medium to long term provides a wealth of data.

often quite adequate, with information that can be compiled later at a higher level in the organisation.

Skills

Familiarity with PME tools and terminology varies greatly: while some organisations are advanced in their practice, learning from others, or through their own experience, others are externally initiated into PME (see Box 4.26). Most challenging are organisations that have been exposed to some ideas and low quality inputs, which may lead to confusion, resistance to new processes and 'de-learning'. Progress with such organisations can only occur after dealing with this confusion and resistance.

Our PME strengthening efforts have highlighted a number of new skills areas necessary to sustain PME processes and these are not only 'technical' in nature. We have found that many of

Box 4.26 PME: What Skills are Needed?

Analysing PME capacity can alert an organisation to a range of skills that are lacking or insufficient. Skills might for example be needed in:

- Data collection and analysis methodologies: appropriate methods, PRA, selection of good sample sizes.
- Documentation and report writing.
- Communication and interviewing.
- Problem analysis; stakeholder analysis.
- Contextual analysis.
- Making strategic choices.

Some of these skills may be relatively new to staff used to implementing activities: where monitoring is restricted to output monitoring, many such skills might be considered superfluous. As we turn to effect- and impact-based monitoring, however, they become more useful. Some can be acquired within the organisation, such as information on optimum sample sizes, or knowledge about the best data collection methods in particular technical fields. Other skills (analytical, communication, interviewing) may need to be developed at a more individual level, as all staff who play a role in PME should ideally have a basic command of these areas.

the skills in short supply among partner organisations can be gained from capacity-building in the field, with guidance and supervision, rather than from formal training. It is in the field that essential communication and interviewing skills, for instance, can best be built up. A learning attitude is, however, indispensable for developing these skills, over and above all the information gathering tools and formats, or the best indicators! We discuss this in the next chapter.

5

PROMOTING LEARNING

While elements of PME systems with a focus on learning often exist in organisations, young and old, we have found that *systematic* organisation-wide learning rarely occurs. There is much mention of the 'learning organisation' among development practitioners, but capacity-building for learning is often directed at individuals, which does not always lead to organisational learning. A learning organisation needs to make use of the experience and knowledge of all its staff and partners, with sound PME and learning practices, policies and systems. This chapter explores our experiences in stimulating such an approach, so that it transcends individual learning and becomes an integral part of organisational culture.

FOSTERING A LEARNING CULTURE

WHEN IS LEARNING 'STUCK'?

Organisational learning requires at the outset a collective recognition of its importance, so that information is accepted as relevant/valid *by everybody*, the outcome of its interpretation becomes *collective* and interventions are believed to be correct *by all* (see Box 5.1). This can require much change in organisational culture: active

Box 5.1 Learning through Experience

ASK, an Indian capacity-building organisation, emphasises learning through experience. All staff, for instance, provide feedback to the director through an annual exercise, a practice introduced because of a national culture where feedback to seniors and elders is rarely acceptable. While the director and top management were committed to openness, informal channels were used by some staff, but others did not have the courage to speak up. A system was therefore devised to help all staff participate and ensure that the director is informed of everyone's views about his leadership style. This feedback is provided in an open meeting with each staff writing positive feedback and areas for improvement on anonymous slips of paper. These are then read out, a discussion facilitated by a senior colleague and an agenda for the director's self-improvement developed. All staff receive similar feedback from everyone. This has created an atmosphere of openness and helps in conducting 360 degree appraisals.

ASK also emphasises the analysis of clients' feedback followed by quick action. It organises bi-monthly exercises to share problems, questions, experiences and distil learning from them. It also looks for opportunities to get its work assessed by external experts by way of evaluations. ASK has thus been able to distance itself from its own work, to review it critically and to innovate policies and practices where necessary.

These innovations include having alternate monthly staff meetings with different agenda (one to review the administrative functioning, the next to share experiences and discuss macro-policy issues); changes in the evaluation methodology; refining the internal mentoring system and developing guidelines on transparency and accountability within ASK and towards outsiders.

participation of all staff, for instance, is not always appreciated by the management or board, and 'learning' is then restricted to a privileged few. Learning is also often informal and undocumented and decisions are taken by the management on the basis of their learning alone, leaving out other colleagues' experiences.

While we are all naturally inclined to learn, there is a strong belief that something (no matter its name) must be done 'to learn'. Where and how learning occurs will, however, depend much more on, say, how meetings are conducted, or on what examples are set by the organisation leadership, in other words, on organisational culture. Without an empowering culture, in which mistakes can be made and even appreciated, and without sound PME systems and practices promoted across the organisation, organisation-wide learning is unlikely to occur. This can best happen when several factors, often combined, are present. We review these in turn.

WORKING ON STAFF ATTITUDES AND ORGANISATIONAL CULTURE

The learning style of organisations varies greatly. Some are focused on action, rather than reflection. Others are keener to learn from other organisations than from their own experiences. Some emphasise effectiveness, efficiency and accountability: they are constantly on the lookout for deficiencies and address them at the earliest opportunity. They have strong institutionalised monitoring systems that include both formal and informal practices. Such organisations keep a constant eye on strategies and results, and regularly change according to their analysis of what works, what does not and what might work better still.

For every proactive organisation, there is often another, with a reactive style of learning, unable to recognise the need to change with time, let alone ahead of it. This is when an organisation undergoes a major overhaul, drastically modifies its approach, or reinvents structure and systems (see Box 5.2). This happens when continuing in the old mode is no longer possible and stakeholders, often donors, raise the alarm. While some organisations survive the crisis, others collapse, or acquire a totally new shape, after painful and expensive change.

Yet other organisations continue to perform at an average level and survive for a while. Not every organisation desires to excel in

Health service staff regularly collect much data, according to pre-established procedures. While this involves many indicators and meticulous records, it is striking how little of this is used for learning purposes. Instead, data is sent to higher levels in the health hierarchy without much internal reflection. If this is understandable for routine activities, where learning is perhaps not essential, it is unfortunate for more innovative activities, for making health services more customer friendly, improving access for poorly served groups, or developing strategies to tackle new diseases. Not using such data also deprives staff from important information about the success of their work, as if learning can only take place at higher levels.

Because of this ingrained perception, the potentially empowering effect of using data for their own needs did not occur to the staff we worked with. This was a lost opportunity, especially for NGOs that claim to be innovative, but get caught in subcontracting arrangements for strictly defined service delivery.

As facilitators, we then had to emphasise the need to look at the vision/mission of the NGOs, which summarised the specific changes they wanted to achieve for their beneficiaries. This helped staff realise that they had neglected their dreams over the years and greatly stimulated a discussion on improving M&E for learning, and to reflect this vision/mission.

its field, especially when the local environment is not competitive. Others are even so opposed to learning that they have a short, or ineffective, life. The working culture then works against exploiting people's potential, with work seen as a 9-to-5 job, without further commitment (see Box 5.3). Such coasting along clearly undermines any wish to use PME for analysis, improvement and learning.

The less the ability to change, the greater the resistance to PME. Our partner's perception of the purpose of PME, whose clarification stands, as we have seen, at the core of the initial steps of a PME support process, signals their motivation to learn. Where PME is seen by staff as a way to check on them, defensive attitudes are expected, rather than an appreciation of PME as a vehicle for learning and for enhanced effectiveness and efficiency.

This ability to change depends on other factors too: larger and older organisations, where practices and systems are entrenched, will find change difficult. They may have many employees eager to

Box 5.3 Challenging a Limited Desire to Excel

An organisation in India's Jharkhand Province had enjoyed a good name, earning credibility through its work on aspects of self-rule and sustainable agriculture with small ethnic groups. It, however, later became self-satisfied, quite oblivious to the modest results it achieved and to the new concepts and practices being used in the region. It learnt insufficiently from its own efforts, could not adapt to the changes taking place in the local context and was unaware of the competition that caught up and surpassed it. The organisation then faced much pressure to develop the quality of its PME and its interventions.

Paradoxically, this pressure resulted in the positive response the PME facilitators later received from the leaders and staff of the organisation. A complete process of renewal could then start, first with some honest admissions of current limitations. For this, the facilitators adopted a non-threatening, but challenging posture: they could understand reasons for past shortcomings, but could not accept these as justification for not changing. A contextual analysis, a redefinition of the vision and the mission, new plans and capacity-building for execution and monitoring followed. These are now slowly, but surely being put into practice.

protect personal interests and fearful of new systems, or practices, such as automation, or PME. Staff may worry that a PME initiative may lead to options that, while good for the organisation, are not in their own interest, such as a transfer to a new location. Managers may also resist change and PME if it threatens their power. At the extreme, where an organisation lacks a sense of accountability and a dedication to development, such as when it is spurred by a financial or other motive that is different from its articulated vision and mission, PME becomes a mere pretext for external consumption.

To understand the learning styles of organisations and to appreciate how they prefer to customise PME systems accordingly, we have found it necessary to identify the strengths and limitations of their current practices, whether learning is proactive or reactive and whether formal or informal mechanisms exist for this. Where we can clarify these aspects at the beginning of our interaction, we can help the organisation recognise its learning style and draw maximum benefit from the facilitation (see Box 5.4). Building on existing practices as much as possible, we can guide it to incorporate elements of critical reflection and combine interventions that will strengthen elements of the culture and systems that foster learning already. This can be stimulated by discussing approaches to learning from our own experiences, presenting cases of organisations that have successfully adopted a learning path and of those that have failed to do so.

Despite these efforts, willingness to change and the desire to excel may still be limited. This will be frustrating for both the facilitator and the partner organisation and lead to tensions, such as when an organisation finds the facilitator too forceful. Conversely, the partner may not be very demanding, perhaps because of low expectations, lack of exposure to competent facilitators, or an element of gratitude if support comes free. We must then adjust the pace and invest in preparatory work before proceeding with PME facilitation. The management of the organisation must at the very least understand the tension that may arise when systematising PME and be willing to tackle it. At this stage, the dialogue can be directed towards striking a balance between individual and organisational priorities. We can stress that learning can lead to personal growth,

Box 5.4 Culture and Shaping Attitudes towards PME

PME support processes recently started with two mid-sized Zambian NGOs and a large faith-based organisation. They had struggled to come to grips with PME without much progress and in spite of donor pressure. The three organisations requested external support, expecting a practical PME system with a set of clever tools and quick techniques to 'solve the problem'.

Reflecting on their current PME practices, it became evident that changing attitudes was a much higher priority: the dominant culture was not oriented towards learning, but towards blaming external factors for failures, such as the recurrent drought, or the beneficiaries' 'resistance to change'. PME was also used as a fault-finding mechanism to help the leaders exert power over colleagues. It was seen as a donor condition for accessing funds and contributed towards seeing all failures as disasters. The leadership did not stimulate critical thinking and learning and the staff hid many 'failures' they knew about.

As facilitators, we first tried to uncover PME-related perceptions, by helping each organisation discuss an example of success and failure from their history. Questions, such as 'Why are these examples of success and failure?' were put to the participants. Different stories were shared, bringing to the surface underlying problems, as well as training needs. We used this to construct a mirror depicting the PME situation, holding it up to the organisations and describing what we saw as outsiders, including issues of culture, attitudes and gaps in skills. Though unpleasant at times, by leaving a door open for dissent, this mirror image gained acceptance. Participants were then asked to suggest behaviours, processes and tools that could be changed with minimal effort and those that would require more input. Commitments made to make any of these changes would then be monitored at the next meeting. We used this 'homework' to assess ownership of the organisation and to motivate the leadership to play their central role. It was a prerequisite for a successful follow-up of the PME process.

The next intervention thus started by monitoring the previous interaction, which helped to underline that PME is a continuous process. Staff discussed what they had been able to change with minimal effort and the factors which had facilitated or hindered change at individual level. Examples included a new, more positive attitude to follow-ups and feedback, better accountability for activities undertaken and increased availability of resources for PME. Much of this was possible, we believe, because of the focus on attitudinal change and leadership commitment, without which any new PME tools cannot be put into meaningful use for real learning.

to the realisation of one's full potential and to drawing satisfaction from this. For the organisation, it will be too late to change gears when the competition has caught up!

LEVELS OF LEARNING AND FOSTERING ANALYSIS

Organisations also differ in their ability to analyse and learn from this analysis: some, for instance, believe in learning from their experiences, but lack the ability to assess themselves. Development workers may implement programmes well, but are not always adept at conceptualising and strategising, so necessary to design effective plans. The rigid application of PME tools and methods also undermines analysis: tools then meet resistance, or are discarded, not because of limited use, but because they are incorrectly applied, or their rationale inadequately explained. Some organisations may also have a subjective view of their work, at times because they wish to impress donors: while presenting an agreeable face to the external world, the ability to remain objective declines and with it the ability to be learning organisations.

To the contrary, when development organisations compete to provide services (such as in providing credit), this encourages a constant analysis of their operations. Training and exposure can also help in developing analytical skills. We have found that explaining the quality of learning by using actual examples from the organisation can serve as a powerful facilitation tool. Thus, once an indicator is monitored and evaluated, or a story listened to, we need to understand what the indicator, or the story, wants to tell us. Measuring the value of indicators is only a first level of analysis, a first step towards learning. We must also ask what this value means and what factors caused the indicator to take this value. Even if this value is as expected, these are useful questions as expected changes might be caused by factors other than those attributable to our interventions. Similarly, looking at averages masks important learning to be drawn from looking at extreme values too! We have now moved to a second level by examining, for instance, more carefully the quality of responses by beneficiaries and whether the choice of activities really contributed to achieving the set objectives. We can then move to a third level, by looking

Box 5.5 Different Levels of Learning

AF is a well-established organisation, working in a drought-prone part of India. From its inception, AF has focused on watershed management, including soil and water management. Technically, the programme stood the test of quality, but sustained results on a wide scale proved elusive for poor farmers. The organisation then moved away from its original technical bias, to include diversification of livelihoods, looking beyond watershed management and rain-fed farming.

Internal learning and reflection were the driving force for this shift, much of it taking place during field visits and staff meetings. Though not formally documented, it was of high quality and helped AF develop its new strategy. Over the years, AF staff also learnt from the land users themselves (see Box 5.9). The table given here illustrates the different levels of analysis and the subsequent action AF envisaged, taking one indicator, the 'quality of maintenance of contour bunds', as an example.

Activity: Construction of earth *bunds* on farmers' fields to control erosion. *Situation:* The indicator highlights maintenance shortcomings. Farmers have ploughed over some *bunds*. What is our analysis? What do we learn and what action may this lead to?

Levels of Learning	Analysis	Action
First level	Poor maintenance caused by farmers' lack of knowledge. We explained the need for proper maintenance while constructing these *bunds*, but they did not pay attention to it or forgot. (Learning sought external reasons. AF's technical quality was beyond doubt.)	Meetings with farmers to repeat the message; extra training to show them how to carry out repairs.

(Box 5.5 Contd.)

(Box 5.5 Contd.)

Second level	Discussing the reasons of poor maintenance with the farmers, we realised that the contour *bunds* in some cases divided their land and made agricultural operations cumbersome. Some sections of *bunds* were superfluous. (Learning now seeks internal reasons, questioning the quality of implementation.)	Involve all farmers in planning the position of *bunds* and incorporate their knowledge. Revise the layout of *bunds* with *bunds* on the field boundaries.
Third level	We discovered that *bunds* are not always the solution: farmers need alternatives to enhance their livelihoods, as rain-fed farming is not promising. (Learning: Original dream of improved watershed management not appropriate. Another dream and strategy needed.)	Seek a more integrated and diversified form of watershed management and farm improvement.

at the relevance of the project, or indeed the relevance of the organisation and its mission.

Conducting M&E in this manner enhances learning, but different persons will reach different conclusions, with different consequences for action. For facilitation purposes, distinguishing different levels of learning and using practical examples (see Box 5.5) helps to demonstrate that the depth of learning can determine different courses of action. Such an exercise can also highlight existing informal knowledge and illuminate to what extent the organisation is self-critical in its analysis of past performance.

KEEPING EYE AND MIND OPEN FOR THE UNEXPECTED

Learning can be enhanced by keeping track of unexpected outcomes and impacts, both positive (as many organisations tend to do) and negative. It is often useful to emphasise the learning dimension of negative experiences and the importance of looking for causes of difficulties internally first instead of blaming external factors. Once an organisation starts to engage in more systematic effect monitoring, surprising unintended effects can emerge. The

Box 5.6 The Unexpected Helps to Learn

✓ Organisations are generally keen and able to discuss unintended effects and impacts. Staff will usually recall them, arising from previous activities, but it is important to elicit both positive and negative examples, as the latter are often downplayed.

✓ The story of an organisation that has undergone a difficult experience, when confronted with a negative and unexpected effect can trigger reflection. Once recounted, such a story can help staff dispel hesitations to share (and laugh about) similar cases from their own history.

✓ Reflecting on such examples helps to communicate the need to constantly adapt PME processes. Unintended effects may imply the need for additional indicators, or even a change in strategy.

✓ We may have to stress that, apart from regular M&E of planned changes, staff should remain alert to other changes in the target group, by asking, for instance, 'What else changed in your life, or in the community?'

character of learning also changes: from individual to group and from a narrow M&E scope on the direct beneficiary group, to the wider community (see Box 5.6 and Chapter 4, section on 'Issues in M&E').

RELATING AND LEARNING

Collaboration between organisations working on similar programmes, or sectors, can provide excellent learning opportunities. When facilitating such learning, we, however, first need to consider the character of the relationships between these organisations—networks, coalitions, alliances, competitors—as they may have different expectations of collaboration and underestimate the costs involved. For learning, collaboration can remain modest with each organisation retaining its distinctive programmes and approach, especially where competition restricts openness. We can stress that learning is not necessarily a matter of establishing which organisation performs better than another.

Second, and often overlooked, each organisation should be encouraged to develop a PME system and practice going beyond output monitoring (see Box 5.7), before joint learning can take place. Third, we have noticed that collaboration for learning works better when started with joint programme planning and identification of appropriate indicators. Once a consensus on such issues is reached, organisations begin to exchange information and experiences on various technical and programme-related topics. Finally, the facilitator needs to take every opportunity to build trust amongst the partners: with confidence, more ambitious combined programmes, or joint problem analysis, can then be envisaged.

LINKING AND LEGITIMISING FORMAL PME AND INFORMAL LEARNING

Field staff usually have a good insight into the results of their work: they observe how situations change for specific groups; learn about these changes and, if expected changes fail to materialise, adapt their approaches. Once staff realise that much of this already entails many PME elements, there is greater acceptance for any PME

Box 5.7 Collaboration as a Learning Mechanism

Five Indian organisations working on a joint initiative to improve livelihoods for marginalised people in remote areas, but implementing their own programme using different approaches, were recently helped to engage in joint learning to improve performance. It was found at the outset that the organisations did not have an appropriate M&E system for such learning and more effort than anticipated had to be invested to develop M&E practices to move the focus from outputs to effects and impact. Each organisation strengthened its M&E in its own way, depending on available resources. With all five organisations well established and with a reputation in their respective area, an open atmosphere for sharing and learning prevailed.

Proactive facilitators were considered essential for this learning process. They managed annual workshops and provided critical PME-related feedback to annual reports. This active role was also necessitated by the physical distance between the five organisations. While each organisation learns within its own setting and collaborates with other organisations nearby, this initiative provided a wider learning platform which they could not efficiently manage on their own. The joint focus on how to learn better and to make informal knowledge more visible, was appreciated by all. One organisation summarised its learning points: a more functional M&E system; a reasonably accurate baseline for effect and impact indicators; a greater understanding of the importance of M&E geared towards effects and impacts and a better learning and self-critical attitude among its staff.

innovation. If informal ways of learning have generated a wealth of experiences, staff will also quickly agree that this knowledge and wisdom is often not visible. A suggestion to bridge this gap through a simple application of PME is then well received. Making their experiences better known and documented demonstrates internal learning and a contribution to higher quality and impact, which in turn fosters interest in PME. It can also stimulate the need for collaboration, for recognising and legitimising informal learning at all levels and for involving and appreciating the contributions of 'junior' staff (see Box 5.8).

Box 5.8 Formal or Informal Learning Mechanisms? Two Cases

A 2003 study of the PME systems of 150 NGOs in India, Tanzania and Peru concluded that all had high quality *formal* activity and output-oriented systems (well-structured, visible, documented and reported on). They all, however, also had largely *informal* PME systems handling information on effects and impacts. This was unstructured, invisible and not reported on. The NGOs were learning informally, but this was by individuals and provided a basis for decisions, but was not systematically brought to the organisational level. The external image of these NGOs was poor, as donor agencies felt that they were not learning. Pointing out this formal–informal divide to staff at the start of a facilitation process helps to create a positive atmosphere and a feeling of confidence. The challenge then becomes clearer: how to make existing informal practices recognised, the unstructured more structured and visible and deciding when such formalisation is desirable.

. Pressed by a donor, an Indian organisation hired an external PME facilitator to conduct planning and monitoring workshops and develop a complete system with staff, emphasising collecting data on activities and results. The facilitator, however, failed to integrate existing monthly reflection meetings which did not use much 'hard' data, but was based on field experiences, community feedback and staff comments. Over the following months, staff grappled with putting in place 'proper' data collection and compilation mechanisms, as advised by the consultant. Any space for open-ended dialogue had, however, vanished and the organisation soon began to feel that while it had data to share with its stakeholders, critical analysis was no longer taking place. Discussions had become mechanical and only focused on reviews of numbers. The facilitator had failed to carry out a thorough PME assessment of formal and informal practices so that a new system reflected this totality. This gap had to be bridged later with a return to open sessions for sharing experiences and reflection, to complement the new system.

LEARNING AND BENEFICIARY PARTICIPATION IN PME

In the Indian programme mentioned earlier, joint staff-community data collection and analysis of effect indicators had unintended effects. One indicator led to the discovery of entirely valid farmer experiments, while discussing others became a catalyst for collective social action (see Box 5.9).

Box 5.9 M&E with Beneficiary Groups Fosters Organisational Learning

A recent review of PME practice in AF, India, demonstrated how joint M&E (with jointly determined indicators) raised learning from individual staff to the wider community. Farmers enthusiastically contributed to this.

We mentioned earlier (Box 4.17) how monitoring the indicator 'water level in the wells' led the community to ban further well drilling in its area. Similarly, using the indicator 'quality of terrace maintenance' led to a discussion among farmers on individual responsibilities and community action. Farmers who did not maintain their terraces were held to account by others. Using the indicator stimulated a sense of common responsibility. It also revealed that one farmer had developed his own maintenance method, which others decided to try and found valuable. Social action had developed as a result of joint monitoring.

The AF staff found this approach contributed to their learning: the discussions on indicators, especially when they took place with the community, broadened their perspective. Learning had also moved from a rather individual matter to a group-based process. It contributed to stronger community relations, bringing people together and extending relations beyond direct beneficiaries to the wider group. The indicators also helped staff attribute effects and impacts to their activities, further enhancing reflection on their relevance and on new action.

This reflected PME facilitation that had progressed from identifying indicators, deciding on monitoring formats and setting out pilot efforts in the field, to building on the open attitude of the staff which, in spite of skills limitations, led to valuable observations. Indeed, 'sub-optimal' indicators stimulated social action in the community. The quality of the reflection process between AF staff and the target groups proved more decisive than very precise indicators.

The development literature lays much emphasis on the participation of beneficiary groups in the PME of programmes or projects (hence the acronym of participatory ME). But theory is often far from practice: we find that such participation is rarely defined as part of a PME system and many of the more top–down donor attitudes with regard to PME are repeated down the aid chain (see Chapter 6). The staff of NGOs then display practices towards their 'partner' communities that are reminiscent of the criticisms they level at their donors. In many situations too, the focus has shifted to the involvement of beneficiaries in the PME of their own groups, while participation in the PME of the NGO takes a backseat. There is, for a start, a role for PME facilitators to make the NGO understand the difference between these two aspects.

From our perspective, to improve and enrich the learning practices of the organisation, beneficiaries have an essential role to play as the key stakeholders. Their insights (such as on unintended changes) are vital for improving the quality of work and practically all development organisations recognise that such participation is desirable in all PME steps. From an ethical perspective too, beneficiaries must have a say in what is being planned in their name. They have a right to comment on the relevance, quality and effectiveness of the services provided to them, on whether the change has had an impact on their lives, and from a wider perspective, on the strategies used for 'their development'.

This is not a new discussion, but, while various methods and tools are available to foster beneficiary participation, there are many gaps in practice. A clear agreement as to what exact role beneficiaries should play and how precisely they can enrich PME processes rarely exists, although, as long as the information needs of both beneficiaries and implementing organisation coincide, the former are generally willing to contribute. If needs are different, however, compensation (such as payment) needs to be provided: we have earlier mentioned the abuse that can arise when beneficiaries execute a task that is the responsibility of a development organisation, such as data collection. Community 'participation' is then seen by staff as saving their time.

Beneficiary needs should largely determine their role in the PME process, such as planning, data gathering, joint determination of indicators, analysis of data, as well as in the PME procedures for the organisation itself. We often find participation at the planning stage, even though it is frequently considered time consuming. At the M&E stage, however, notably in data collection, analysis and especially in decision-making, practice becomes less widespread. Although we have experienced good results with the joint identification and appreciation of indicators, we rarely see local people meaningfully involved in M&E. External participation in analysing data is often said to be difficult and rarely happens, especially when field staff are themselves not much involved. Yet, where a concerted effort has been made, beneficiary participation in analysis has proved easy to organise and has yielded high quality information.

As PME facilitators, we can insist that beneficiary participation in PME be decided as policy and that institutional mechanisms to guarantee this participation be established. This is especially useful in larger NGOs where, for instance, a central office is far from communities and PME, while allowing the community to participate in 'grass-roots processes' to some extent, excludes their views from the central PME NGO level. All these issues, and their resource implications, can be reviewed while helping the partner organisation develop, or update, its PME policy.

ENHANCING THE ACCEPTANCE OF 'FINANCIAL PME'

Where there is some wariness for PME, this is especially so with its financial dimension. Non-finance staff often view financial issues as uninteresting, or only of concern to accountants and general managers who deal with 'accountability' to boards and outside parties. Such lack of appreciation can be quite evident in development organisations, where the finance department often operates in isolation. Such views can, in our experience, be tackled in four main ways:

TEAMWORK BETWEEN FINANCE AND PROGRAMME STAFF

To have others appreciate finance and accounting, finance staff need to work with their programme or field colleagues. The skills of finance staff are after all meant to promote efficiency and to provide the management information needed to improve the quality of M&E taking place elsewhere in the organisation (see Box 5.10). Any meaningful programme evaluation must therefore review the programme's cost-effectiveness and only such teamwork can lead to full evaluation at the output, effect and impact levels. We can facilitate the involvement of both staff categories in activity planning, budgeting, financial and internal controls, reporting and auditing (see Box 5.11).

Box 5.10 Integrity of Accounts and Culture Change

In large NGOs in Angola, facilitators have helped institute a culture of shared responsibility for the integrity of accounts between programme and accounting staff. The accounting department issues a complete monthly report detailing all account entries made to various departments and project acccunts against their respective budgets. Heads of departments and project managers are responsible for checking these reports for unauthorised, or incorrect bookings, and send their comments to the accounting department for a further check.

As facilitators, we noted that such a culture change towards teamwork between programme and accounting staff helps to:

- Improve analysis, based on integrity of financial information.
- Monitor and evaluate budgets against actual expenditure.
- Achieve programme objectives cost-effectively.
- Integrate activity and financial reporting.

PARTICIPATORY RESULT-ORIENTED PLANNING AND BUDGETING

This can involve all staff in the organisation and will anticipate the cost information needed to allow for evaluations in which activity and financial cost reporting are integrated. We have found that, when planning and budgeting are managed as an organisational process, all staff become more cost-conscious in achieving their objectives. Second, when this is conducted within a clear organisation structure,

In a recent exercise to facilitate the development of programme and financial PME systems in an Indian NGO, two facilitators (one for programmes, the other for finance) worked separately with the programme and financial staff, as provided for in their terms of reference. Work schedules and timelines were also prepared separately and, although the host organisation had planned a common meeting with both facilitators, this did not materialise.

In contrast, the same facilitators worked as a team to help programme and financial planning with other NGOs working on tsunami rehabilitation projects. The results proved to be remarkably different, as joint work led to a better synchronisation of the programme and finance functions. Finance plans and budgets were prepared in relation to programme plans and could be detailed to specific allocations thanks to clarity on the types of activities involved. Programme and financial progress could also be plotted together with regard to reporting systems, making monitoring more informative and corrective actions more logical. This was highlighted at a workshop which brought together the programme and finance staff of the NGOs and was led by programme and finance facilitators working in tandem. Planning discussions were followed by the preparation of result-based budgeting and a monitoring and reporting framework. The programme reporting format borrowed columns on 'budget allocations' and 'actual expenditures' and placed them alongside the 'results planned' and 'results achieved' columns. The NGO participants could then clearly see the link between programme and financial progress.

it also becomes a management instrument that enables staff to accept accountability not only for the outputs of 'their' activities, but also for the effects that these outputs have on achieving higher organisation objectives. This enhances their motivation and acts as a stepping-stone towards involvement in other forms of decision-making. Participation by the beneficiary group in the budgeting process can also increase impact by including their definition and indicators of success.

These benefits can only arise if decision-making is sufficiently delegated to staff, or other stakeholders, and if organisational strategies and objectives are clear to them. Management must also be transparent as to who is held responsible for important organisational functions and provide monitoring information to the 'budget implementers' so that they can steer towards better results.

TRANSPARENT COST ALLOCATION

Connecting planning and budgeting with the accounting function requires a transparent cost-allocation system, which identifies: (a) the 'direct costs' of each activity, project, programme and organisation-wide costs, such as office rent, or depreciation, (b) 'indirect support costs' for support units and administration to be added to the direct costs as a first part of overheads and (c) 'indirect coordination costs' such as director's costs to be added to the direct costs as a second layer of overheads. A cost report, showing the entire cost-structure of a programme, or organisation, should include all these elements. A cost-allocation system is transparent

Box 5.12 Transparent Cost Allocation Step-by-step

In Ethiopia, a number of consultancies with an NGO gradually introduced PME systems and practices. In finance, the first step with a planning and budgeting system focused on introducing activity-based accounting, allowing planning and accounting for the direct costs of each programme.

This was appreciated as very worthwhile by the NGO, but it took time to convince the staff of the need to continue with a full-fledged cost-allocation system. As facilitators, we had to highlight the need, for a large NGO with various activities and products, to (a) establish full cost price for their products, or services and (b) integrate activity with financial reporting. To do both successfully required allocating all costs, including support, overhead and depreciation costs, to all activities and programmes. It was important to demonstrate that, however time-consuming such a process may be, it is essential to provide the information required for meaningful evaluation and learning.

when the whole system has been documented, kept up-to-date and external auditors have verified its correct implementation in their annual report (see Box 5.12).

Cost allocation then provides the information required for effective evaluation at the main activity or programme level. It includes, for example, evaluation of the cost-effectiveness of achievements, bearing in mind, however, that cost-effectiveness is not cost-efficiency, as the lowest cost is not necessarily the best. Partner organisations often hesitate to focus on cost-efficiency or effectiveness and react defensively when asked about this. Nevertheless, such a focus can be a powerful aspect of PB(udgeting)ME, to strengthen teamwork between finance and other departments and to deepen learning within the organisation.

CONTRIBUTING TO ORGANISATIONAL SUSTAINABILITY

Finally, we have found that a good understanding of the role of financial policies and strategies in building the overall organisation can also enhance an appreciation of financial PME. Since donors usually restrict the use of their funds to a particular project, it is important for the organisation to ensure that this can be accounted for through well-documented and transparent internal controls. But organisational sustainability includes financial sustainability, even financial stability. Two financial strategies underpin this:

1. **Charging fair and transparent overhead costs:** Development organisations often need to improve their negotiation skills in dealing with donors and other parties interested in their products and services. This requires financial information that is not based on donor/financier needs, but on internal management needs. Financial reporting should in the first place be to oneself and of a wider nature than donor-reporting, which is a secondary need. We can help partner organisations negotiate so that donor reporting fits their activity structure as much as possible and so that donors and other 'customers' pay for most overhead costs, on the basis of a fair and transparent cost-allocation system (see Box 5.13). Not having such a system provides a valid excuse for donors and others to refuse paying their fair share of overhead costs that no quality

Box 5.13 Helping Donors Accept to Pay their Fair Share of Partners' Overhead Costs

Most donors find it difficult to pay for their partners' overhead costs. For young, or weaker organisations, this often means dependence on one friendly donor to pay all overheads. Better established organisations, which generate some of their 'own' income, are expected to use this income to cover such costs and then miss the opportunity to use it to strengthen their organisation, or otherwise enhance the impact of their work.

As a facilitator with several East African NGOs, after talking to donor and partner organisations, a first step was to help both parties understand each other's prejudices: most NGOs believe that donors will never change their mind and that there is no point in trying. Talking to the donors, we found that the refusal to pay for overheads stemmed from the fear of being 'overcharged' because of a lack of transparency as to what these costs really amounted to. So we assisted the NGOs to negotiate with their donors to use as much of their 'own' non-donor income as possible to develop their own financial sustainability. This, in effect, required the donor to agree and pay for overhead costs. Having demonstrated to both the NGO and the donor that a transparent system of charging overhead costs could be produced, both parties agreed on the validity of such a system.

Frank discussions between donors and their partners in several other countries encouraged others to follow suit. Both parties also agreed that more donors would accept to pay for their share of overheads once partner organisations were able to show in their reports that overhead costs remain at reasonable levels and that all donors are asked to pay their fair share of such costs. This removes donor fears that 'clever' organisations can 'make a profit' on charging overheads because of poor controls and documentation. With the assistance of the donor, several organisations developed a transparent cost-allocation and reporting system and asked their external auditors to verify in their annual audit report that project charges had been implemented accordingly.

Since then, signs are that some donors are willing to follow suit, while more hesitant ones run the risk of seeing better established NGO partners refuse to implement projects with them in the future. Non-governmental organisations that have developed such transparent cost reports have created a more equal relationship with donors, enhanced their negotiating skills and managed their own affairs more efficiently and with greater effect, even beyond individual projects.

product, or project, can do without. We return to negotiating donor conditions in the next chapter.

2. **Securing maximum financial stability and more 'developmental funding' from donors:** This does not receive much attention, possibly because development organisations tend to look at donor funding as their main strategy. With stability in mind, this attitude can be replaced by a clear financial strategy, to be managed by board, management and staff. Such a strategy can include cost-efficiency policies and procedures, building up a 'stability reserve fund' to a predetermined level, ensuring replacement of fixed assets without donor assistance and securing adequate human resources for financial management. It also entails reporting an informative balance sheet, managing it towards a desired

structure with adequate fund levels, seeking other funds (such as cost recovery where appropriate) and negotiating with donors for more 'developmental' funding policies as we illustrate in the next chapter.

STIMULATING OWNERSHIP AND PARTICIPATION IN PME: IMPLICATIONS FOR THE FACILITATOR

SHARPENING OUR ORGANISATIONAL ANALYSIS

What immediate obstacles might we confront when requested to facilitate the improvement or introduction of PME, with a learning focus? A thorough assessment of obstacles *at the outset* will depend on our previous experiences and knowledge of a partner organisation and its context, as well as the opportunity of influencing its leadership.

Occasionally, opportunism, the total absence of a learning culture, or donor impositions might be 'killer obstacles'. Opportunistic behaviour is not a concern in itself, but an organisation that seeks donor funding regardless of whether this fits with its vision/mission will have a restricted, project-focused view on its PME needs. If a sense of accountability is also lacking, the PME facilitator will have to explore if the departure from the organisation's motive is unintentional and can be corrected. Only then can we proceed. Second, where there is only interest in a system to control and blame people (usually a concealed agenda), there is little a facilitator can do. Third, where donor-imposed systems obstruct learning and are not negotiable, one can do little. Opportunities to bring together the PME requirements of different stakeholders therefore also need to be checked before starting.

Other complications are more common, such as when an organisation is reluctant to invest in PME because of financial crisis, is without a coherent programme, lacking vision, mission, or a clear internal structure to guide implementation. Also common are organisations that struggle to integrate their PME into external government systems, or those experiencing strained relations with beneficiaries because of limited results on the ground. Some of these obstacles can be surmounted with a good explanation of what PME entails, or by spending time on strategic planning to reach a minimum of coherence and shared vision. Without such a step, subsequent PME support would rest on a weak foundation.

NECESSARY MIND SHIFTS

To promote learning, mind shifts may be needed for a partner to meet the organisational requirements described in this chapter. The PME facilitator is likely to meet resistance, especially when working with partners that espouse a more technocratic outlook, as mind shifts require personal change in the first place. The major changes include:

1. **Moving from project-oriented to organisation-wide PME:** This might not appear so radical if reference is made to existing internal (administration, finance) monitoring and to any formal, or informal, context monitoring. Managers will then realise that they already practise organisation-wide PME. We can also help partners to develop a larger picture of their reality, such as through exchange visits, or case studies.

2. **Improving effect and impact monitoring:** This may require considerable investment, implications might be difficult to define and there might be a fear of information overkill. Effect and impact M&E will present organisations with unexpected effects, which will require reviews and corrections. Stressing the linkage with existing informal processes in the organisation helps to lower such fears.

3. **Being transparent:** This may be challenging. When informal learning is prevalent, leaders can maintain their position, while a more formalised learning system may require a different, more open, self-confident leadership. Enlisting support from other stakeholders (for example, board members) before facilitating processes to promote learning mechanisms may be useful here, as well as confronting poor learning practices.

4. **Integrating PME in daily tasks and resource allocation:** Acknowledging that PME-related tasks, including any informal learning, already constitute part and parcel of a daily routine contributes to acceptance. Some of the tips mentioned under

resourcing a PME cycle (see Chapter 4) apply here, as well as the elaboration of PME calendars (see Chapter 4, section titled 'Timing: PME Calendars'). Once PME becomes an integral part of staff tasks, work planning and resource allocation should become more flexible.

5. **Assigning appropriate roles and responsibilities to all persons involved in PME:** This is also important for ownership and participation. We have noted that data collection and analysis should not be separated. Ignoring field staff contributions, for instance, undermines ownership of PME processes. We have also noted that, while specialist M&E persons can play an important role in supporting a PME building process in an organisation, they should refrain from implementation, giving the impression that their role is to check on others and distancing PME tasks from field staff.

DESIGNING A LONG-TERM, STEP-BY-STEP INCLUSIVE SUPPORT PROCESS

Given the need for such mind shifts, PME strengthening becomes a long-term process requiring flexible facilitators, able to adapt to new situations. Time and cost-effectiveness are also of the essence, to avoid wasting energy in organisations confronting many obstacles to change. Honesty is also necessary, especially when the partner's response is inadequate. That is the time to clarify our stance and to negotiate the next steps: actions by our partner must follow our inputs.

Working with an entire organisation, or at least a good cross-section of its staff, fosters a broad acceptance of PME and organisation-wide learning. Joint sessions for field visits with beneficiaries also stimulate collective learning. Our experiences in identifying indicators with a beneficiary community, with staff impressed by local knowledge and clarity in expression, illustrate this. Such interaction also encourages internal debates where staff can question the relevance of previous capacity-building activities that were more individually oriented or detached from the field (see Box 5.14).

Gradually building PME into existing programmes, instead of waiting for a new phase, also eases acceptance. Taking existing programmes as starting points without changing their design fits

Box 5.14 It Takes Time and Effort: Institutionalising Learning

Pradan works in several Indian regions to promote livelihoods for the rural poor. More than 200 staff support 100,000 families, organised into 6,000 women's self-help groups involved in microfinance. As a Pradan colleague explains, with expansion, an internal learning system (ILS) became necessary: 'Experiences over the years helped us realise that our ILS had to balance information needs for "proving" to our external and internal constituents and learning for the community, staff and ourselves. In Pradan's ILS, each individual member, self-help group and staff provides information that makes up systematic data on indicators at different levels (output/effects/ impacts). At the same time each contributor to the process reflects, evaluates progress and plans for future improvements.'

Three lessons were learnt. First, 'The institutionalisation of the ILS depended on building ownership by staff and clients since, at the end of the day, they have to use it to produce useful information and learn for themselves: the system had to address their requirements first, before answering questions of importance to management. Both therefore had to be extensively involved in its design. An important consensus that was reached after consultations was that the ILS should have livelihoods as an important theme. A large portion of individual and group diaries (or "workbooks") were therefore devoted to analysis of income and expenditure in the family, ownership of resources, and planning for their optimal use. These workbooks are sequentially arranged, customised for different levels and the internal logic connecting the different levels worked out. They are a curriculum for self-development. This was a departure from earlier practice, where the system mostly dealt with impact indicators. The ILS would not just be a reflective tool, but would be a tool for "reflective action". Field testing offered a reality check as to the level of details needed, the best indicators for maximum learning and the methods needed to introduce pictorial workbooks.

Second, a guiding concern was that the ILS should not become a set of formats added to the heavy workload of the field staff. It had to be institutionalised, meshed with day-to-day operations. An aspect that is constantly highlighted about the ILS is therefore that it does not reduce time commitments in the field, but helps make time spent more fruitful. Staff have found the ILS set of modules useful not only for routine data collection, but the use of pictures gave it enormous versatility that turned it into a training tool as well, and a means to standardise group facilitation.

(Box 5.14 Contd.)

(Box 5.14 Contd.)

> Third, above all, an enabling environment had to exist within Pradan, with finer processes and concerns, not just hard-core numbers, valued. Once this was created, the system could be introduced in a participatory manner. This has helped the ILS make a large contribution to Pradan's work, with both useful client feedback and impact information now available.'

well with the learning dimension of PME, with previous plans considered as given and learning used to generate information to review the next stage.

FOSTERING ACCOUNTABILITY

Development organisations need to distinguish between outputs, for which they are accountable, and effects and impacts, for which they may feel accountable, but whose achievement is not entirely in their hands. Asking which results and corresponding resources the organisation can be held accountable for can help staff reflect on the logical relation between what they do and how they can reasonably expect their beneficiaries to use these outputs. Staff can then review the relevance of the objectives set and whether the implemented activities are appropriate to lead to these objectives. They can then adjust their often ambitious and vague objectives to a more realistic level. This downward accountability for results to the beneficiaries comes first, only complementing other dimensions of accountability, to donors and colleagues, which are usually emphasised. Facilitating a discussion on accountability in relation to the result level often proves rewarding and does not require much time (see Box 5.15). Once the logical story line, connecting

Box 5.15 Visualising Levels of Accountability

- ✓ Levels of accountability can be visualised by drawing a 1–10 scale on the ground and asking participants to stand on the point of the scale corresponding to the level of accountability they feel for a particular output.
- ✓ The exercise can be repeated for other outputs, effects and impacts. Differences between staff can be used to facilitate discussion and reflection.

activities and outputs with desired changes has been developed, staff will quickly grasp the implications on their responsibilities for results.

ENHANCING CONVERGENCE BETWEEN INTERNAL AND EXTERNAL INFORMATION REQUIREMENTS

Donors' information requirements on effects and impacts are often very similar to those of the partner organisation. This goes against the conventional perception that stresses divergent needs, forcing organisations to collect information they do not need. Such assumed divergence is often caused by poorly formulated questions by donor agencies, or different interpretations of terminology and concepts, rather than different needs. Recognising this convergence stimulates ownership of a PME system as there is no need to artificially build a completely different system. This, however, requires the organisation to position itself clearly, to have a well-formulated PME policy and an ability to negotiate information requirements with its donors. Donors, however, constitute only one of the actors in the wider environment of a development organisation that will have an influence on its PME practice. The next chapter focuses on this broader context.

6

THE BROADER CONTEXT: PME CHALLENGES AND RESPONSES

Development organisations do not operate in isolation: they are subject to many external forces. While they may influence some of these, they have little influence over many others. This chapter looks at the importance of this wider context for organisations developing and using a PME system. We have found analysing this dynamic context challenging, which partly explains why it often receives little attention and why trends are often assumed rather than monitored. We describe working on contextual aspects that often matter, keeping in mind that every context is unique and constantly changing. These aspects include PME and the broad cultural context, with an emphasis on gender issues, relationships with other NGOs and interacting with donors, including the PME-related concepts that frequently accompany them.

DEALING WITH CULTURAL ISSUES

Culture expresses itself in various ways–as practices, norms and values adopted by different people, groups and communities–and at different levels, international, national and local. Culture also varies in other ways: the non-profit sector has its distinct features, but considerable differences exist among development organisations. Culture also stems from and results in different patterns of distribution of power, which influence mindsets. Some notions then become dominant and are later taken as 'natural', such as beliefs about change, its nature and its desirability. In facilitating PME, many issues linked to culture spring to mind: is the cultural context favourable to change? Is it open or closed? Are people stimulated to learn? Does the government promote accountability? What is the place of women, leaders and religion and how do these aspects affect PME? Whatever the context, a number of cultural factors are relevant to the practice of PME and its facilitation:

COMMUNICATION CULTURE

Communication influences PME practice. In some societies, asking questions suggests mistrust, in others interest. Requiring written information may be interpreted as a sign of impending criticism and in some countries the word 'monitoring' has a policing, even military connotation. Thus, while a donor may feel that a 'monitoring visit' is a factual description of intent, a partner organisation may interpret this quite differently (see Box 6.1). Even religious beliefs can influence people's attitudes towards communication: members of a tight-knit religious community may, for instance, feel that it is not necessary to have a written PME system, given their prevailing mutual trust.

Political systems may foster freedom of speech, or repress deviant opinions. Openly criticising the way civil servants treat the public may, for instance, not be acceptable in a closed political environment, where people are expected to adhere to the predominant ideology when speaking about planning and programme results, thus limiting the scope for transparent PME practice. In some countries, civil society organisations are closely supervised by the government, with

Box 6.1 Culture, M&E and Financial Accounting

Strengthening financial accounting in partner organisations is rarely only a 'technical' job. One reason is that accounting comes close to the core of national culture. Thus:

✓ Whereas financial accounting is usually presented as a quasi-scientific subject, it can assume a strong political connotation, especially in situations of acute scarcity of resources. With scarcity, control over funds becomes associated with power, and access seen as a privilege, rather than an entitlement.

✓ Financial accounting can reflect gender roles. In many community organisations, women hold the post of treasurer, having often proved to be more reliable in handling money than their male counterparts.

✓ Such factors may lead to conflict: open financial information is not always easy to nurture, as transparency may not be in everybody's interests. Asking questions about expenditure can be interpreted as a sign of mistrust.

✓ This cultural dimension also influences planning and budgeting. In the South, money is sometimes spent soon after it becomes available, as opposed to the more bureaucratic approaches advocated in the North, rigidly dictated by plans and budgets.

strict rules and regulations, which restrict freedom of expression. Where insecurity and oppression limit people's ability to speak, an open PME system is dangerous for those involved in acts that are not permitted. Organisations working in such situations are weary of recording information and necessarily work on trust. Thus many Latin American NGOs, working under oppressive regimes in the 1970s and 1980s developed two separate identities, one official and another hidden, used when working with refugees, or the political opposition. Where written information is too risky, alternatives must be developed to communicate, including special arrangements with donors on the type of information they can receive.

Where the political system promotes decentralisation combined with an open atmosphere, on the other hand, possibilities for joint PME and agreements on indicators and results between development organisations and local governments can thrive, although where decentralisation takes the form of government subcontracting community organisations or other NGOs, this is often accompanied by mandatory PME systems.

Cultural factors influence the type of leaders we find in development organisations and their interaction with their environment affects PME. Culture can, for instance, foster open or closed management styles, can produce leaders who are considered all-knowing or open to criticism, in turn facilitating change or slowing it down. The mere presence of a leader during a planning meeting can, for instance, affect its results (see Box 6.2). Age, as a dimension of leadership, also varies with the cultural context. In many African and Latin American communities, age is much valued–and the opinion of older people often considered decisive. In other contexts, advanced age is disregarded and power attributed to younger people.

Knowledge about leadership in a partner organisation helps to design a PME system. Choices have to be made, for instance, to balance the involvement of different groups (or their representatives) to tackle distrust and make a PME system fair and effective (see Box 6.3). Procedures for information gathering may be facilitated by structuring it, for example, by dividing informants into age or gender groups. Indicators may similarly need to be differentiated.

Box 6.2 The Fear to Disclose Information

When a donor insisted that its partner organisation, a Philippino NGO, adopt a new approach to PME, with participatory M&E and a planning system with success indicators, it was assumed that a culture of open discussions prevailed, with all staff seeking honest answers as to why certain plans had been successfully implemented and others had not.

This new approach, which included a strong re-planning mechanism based on M&E outcomes, only worked well in part and was especially difficult with regard to M&E. Defensive attitudes rather than openness prevailed. The facilitator had first convened a meeting of field staff and bookkeepers who jointly evaluated results at the field level. Various conclusions were drawn, some critical of management practices. At a subsequent session with management and field staff, the latter did not dare to bring up these up. When the facilitator quoted some and managers started querying them, field staff refuted them, implying that these were the facilitator's conclusions.

National and organisational cultural values stood in the way of frank evaluative questions. While the planning process was in tune with a national culture that emphasises a long-term orientation, the approach to M&E was more alien, possibly because avoidance of uncertainty is not so important in this context (including whether one can ascertain that achievements result from one's own activities). Culture also made criticising the boss in open meetings unacceptable. Added to an organisational culture where monitoring was seen as a way to identify those making errors, we can see why defensive behaviour crept into the M&E process that was being introduced.

A facilitator who is aware of such cultural values can avoid many pitfalls. By openly discussing how culture and organisational behaviour may impede learning, appropriate practices can be encouraged in the organisation.

Box 6.3 Opting for Standards of Accountability and Performance in a Culture where Individual Freedom is much Prized

Reach Manipur works for peace and development among two Indian ethnic groups with a history of armed conflict and a strong belief in egalitarianism and individual freedom. The staff and board consist of equal numbers of both groups. Although the staff usually do their best at work, they often feel uncomfortable asking and being asked questions about their performance and results, as this is not a usual practice in the local cultural context.

At a recent strategy workshop, the board members and staff went into protracted discussions on PME practice, but finally agreed to set standards of performance and developed strategies to help staff overcome the deep-rooted inhibitions that emanate from their culture.

The PME process is now taking root, with emphasis on accountability and learning, but situations have arisen where staff have had to be reminded of the norms they developed to ensure accountability. Slow but steady progress has been made, and the culture of accountability is setting in, despite the contextual challenge. The key for the facilitator was to acknowledge this uniqueness, bring it up for discussion and set a realistic time line for implementation.

ORAL AND WRITTEN CULTURE

Many societies have a strong oral tradition, making a written PME system challenging, especially among beneficiary groups with low literacy levels. This has obvious consequences for the way information must be handled and may affect the capacity of organisations to communicate, for example, with donor, or government agencies, that usually require written information. Reliance on the written words may also be variously interpreted in different cultural contexts: as a sign of seriousness in taking into account what is being said, or as limited trust. Yet, because of distance and time constraints, development work increasingly relies

Box 6.4 Informal but Precise Monitoring Tools

✓ A traditional monitoring tool in Uganda: 'When growing up, I saw children being weighed on hospital scales. This prompted me to ask my mother: "Before the days of scales, how did you monitor child growth?" So she explained: one week after the umbilical cord fell off, the mother would tie pieces of banana fibre or strings made from bark around the waist and wrists. As the child grew, the strings would become tight, forcing the mother to replace them with bigger ones. She would count the number of lunar cycles the string stayed. Whenever it would take too long to outgrow the strings, she would consult older women for advice. Nowadays, some mothers use beads instead of bark strips, which adds beauty to the monitoring tool' (a PME facilitator from Uganda).

✓ Multi-stakeholder participation and early warning systems: East African governments have established early warning systems (EWS) for their arid and semi-arid areas to warn of imminent droughts and to monitor climate changes. Local communities also have their EWS by observing natural phenomena and the behaviour of animals. They closely monitor market prices for meat and grains, as this determines the time to sell their animals. Often neglected in the past, it is now recognised that, for relevance and acceptance, EWS must incorporate these informal community systems, which enrich and add 'ground truth' to the 'scientific' ones. Non-governmental organisations play an important role in several countries to integrate local systems in wider EWS.

Box 6.5 Written and Unwritten PME

✓ Project reporting for the Subanen people in the Philippines: Project reporting for the Subanen people in the Philippines had been problematic, as their health and agricultural project is implemented by an organisation of indigenous peoples, where oral traditions prevail and literacy is below 50 per cent. Regular programme and context reviews had been carried out by the community of 23 villages through story telling among women and elders, most of whom cannot read and write. The findings were then transmitted through the village social structures. This made monitoring progress difficult for external supporters. As the project aimed at helping local groups advocate to reclaim their ancestral domain, it was essential that community processes be shared with their allies, including donors. Facilitators then helped to build a PME process that combined oral tradition with process documentation. Reviews now take place by means of stories, but this is documented by project staff. The project director delivers an annual report to the community elders through stories, but a written version is prepared for external supporters.

✓ A pictorial approach to PME to strengthen gender equity: Pradan works in some of India's poorest regions. It supports a broad livelihoods approach, with a focus on women's self-help groups. As part of its learning system, Pradan developed pictorial workbooks to strengthen client learning, to make impact assessment routine and to monitor social performance. These books are designed around sets of indicators relevant to group members: well-being, financial security and livelihood, empowerment and participation. A member looks at each picture (a happy or sad woman, for instance), reflects on how that indicator applies to her and places a mark according to her current status. She revisits the picture periodically to assess changes and to plan improvement vis-à-vis that indicator, if required. Using this approach, women were observed to adopt a reflective mode and lead the discussions on many previously unspoken issues. These are often followed up by the women, with evident action. This is, however, a process-intensive tool with required much 'buy-in' among Pradan staff to be fully accepted. Staff who have used the approach report that, with time, facilitation skills develop, thus reducing the field work needed. Some staff members are also devising their own pictorial modules to address specific needs.

(Box 6.5 Contd.)

(Box 6.5 Contd.)

✓ Using video for programme monitoring in India: Development organisations increasingly use videos to monitor activities. A video helps to record an activity in motion such as a training event, a micro-planning exercise in the village, street theatre and the like for later analysis to assess quality and enhance effectiveness. Video is also used to record village council meetings, cases of lawlessness and dysfunctional village services. Women have been systematically trained for this purpose and their recordings add pressure to conduct meetings effectively, or provide better services. Videos also document other events, such as rallies, or public hearings, and are used to disseminate information.

on writing, rather than face-to-face interactions, with written reports and budgets used to monitor relationships and performance.

Furthermore, PME tools often use English, French, or Spanish, and rarely reflect local language, knowledge and cultural sensitivities. Indigenous languages often have vocabularies and use concepts that do not easily translate into the more formal PME terminology. We then see barriers between NGO staff, who often speak the 'official' language, and the beneficiary group, who speak another. Building a common PME language understood by all then becomes a challenge in itself (see Boxes 6.4 and 6.5).

QUALITATIVE AND QUANTITATIVE DATA

We have noted that development organisations can share a prejudice against qualitative indicators and 'soft' information, preferring 'hard' quantitative data, perceived as more reliable. Beneficiaries, on the other hand, often appreciate qualitative data, such as soil colour as an indication of its fertility, instead of laboratory data on organic matter content. In some cultural contexts, the usage of numbers– and therefore quantified indicators–may be inappropriate. In some African countries, for instance, counting someone's cattle may be interpreted as a first step towards taxing, or even stealing them. A qualitative measure can indeed be as effective as a quantitative one, better adapted to the beneficiaries' reality, cheaper and faster to use.

Education systems can encourage critical thinking and innovation, or emphasise the repetition of information. They can adhere to strict boundaries between disciplines, or stress problem-based and integrative approaches. Access to education can also be highly selective: in many countries, development workers belong to a small elite and find relating on equal terms with their less-formally educated 'beneficiaries' difficult. Access and type of education system shapes the learning culture and therefore PME, including the way information is accessed and used and how results are critically assessed.

Box 6.6 PME and Culture

✓ In some cultural contexts, asking too many 'why?' questions may be interpreted as lack of trust or confidence: instead, inviting descriptions using other prompters, using open questions and sharing examples may be more appropriate. Similarly, drawing comparisons and contrasting cultural contexts can reduce tensions. Well-chosen jokes, especially if they are at the expense of the PME facilitator who authors them, can tame the expert syndrome. Stories can also elicit cultural opportunities and constraints with regard to PME practice.

✓ Facilitators with a thorough understanding of the local cultural context will often have the edge.

✓ Working separately with small homogenous groups—women and men, for instance—can help draw out information and build self-confidence.

✓ We can also encourage those who emphasise the written word (such as donor, or government, representatives) to attend informal community events.

GENDER AND PME FACILITATION

As one of the principal factors determining the place of a person in the household, organisation, community and society, gender affects all aspects of PME, including indicator selection, participation in

PME and communication at PME events (see Box 6.7). We have frequently worked with development organisations paying lip-service to gender equity while challenges persist, in part because 'gender practice' challenges our very own behaviour as development workers and PME facilitators. But positive experiences also exist.

Box 6.7 Culture, Gender and Indicators

Gender differences emerged when we discussed the indicators needed to measure the success of a programme to improve women's incomes with male and female staff in a Paraguayan NGO. This focused on the promotion of traditional textile products, linking producers with external markets. Everybody agreed on the specific objective: improving incomes earned by women entrepreneurs. Female staff noted that they did not mind whether women continued to use traditional patterns and colours; ability to sell was most important. The male staff disagreed: they expected women to follow traditional designs. For them, these constituted the core quality of any improvement in income. Women had adopted a more pragmatic approach, while men struggled to preserve the traditional culture.

This discussion was the result of using the four-question format, as set out in Box 4.4, this volume, on specifying objectives and indicators. As the discussion progressed from being vague at the objective level, to having more precise indicators of success, the different views in the organisation became visible for the first time. As facilitators, we have often found this tool valuable as it forces a clarification of the desirable situation for which staff want to be held accountable and helps the organisation develop its internal coherence.

A Story Leads to a Gender-based Indicator

At a recent PME workshop with staff in a health NGO in Ghana, participants shared stories of hospital practices. One concerned a husband who wished to accompany his wife into the labour room, but was scolded for going to the 'wrong' place. The hospital had adopted the norms of traditional Ghanaian society that stipulate that men have no role to play at the time of birth, which was regarded as strictly a women's affair. As norms evolve, however, the wish of husbands and wives to deliver 'together' conflicts with these practices. Giving gender imbalances such a clear practical form helps organisations rethink their change agenda and establish indicators for such changes. In this example, health staff realised how they too played a negative role and had to change. It also meant that clinics had to adapt their physical layout, with separate labour rooms, allowing fathers to attend deliveries. An indicator would then be the presence and number of such rooms and the number of deliveries taking place there. A seemingly technical indicator thus has institutional and social dimensions, representing a deep change in health institutions, including their approach to gender issues.

A 'Total Organisation Approach' to Gender and PME

An Indian organisation recently facilitated the preparation of gender mainstreaming plans in water users' associations (WUAs) that manage irrigation tanks in the province. The planned results were kept modest because of socio-cultural realities, and envisaged increased awareness among women of their rights and roles in irrigation management. With only one nominated woman in each WUA committee, who often feels hesitant to speak in front of 11 male members, participation hardly occurred. It was clear that several measures had to be taken to get results, reflecting each WUA's socio-economic and cultural situation. These included gender mainstreaming training for all WUA executive committees, joint plan development and revision with WUA leaders and selected women, appointment of a gender mainstreaming worker at each WUA, assured resources for gender mainstreaming and developing a legal framework for the effective participation of women in the WUAs.

While facilitating the development of M&E indicators for an organisation implementing a human rights support programme in Uganda, a participant mentioned 'cases of wife beating reported to the police' as a relevant indicator. He was soon interrupted by a number of 'strong men' in the group: '*Look here, in our culture, wife beating is accepted. Your wife cannot respect you if you are not prepared to beat her*'. Given such attitudes and knowledge gaps (Uganda has signed conventions and laws that protect women), it is unlikely that the organisation will be effective in its field endeavours without first

---

Box 6.8 Gender and PME Facilitation

✓ Given the unique character of any community, it is advisable to begin with a thorough gender analysis exercise, rather than adopt standard measures in the name of gender mainstreaming.

✓ We have often found training for gender mainstreaming throughout the organisation a prerequisite for tackling gender and PME issues. This involves reflecting on organisational values, working with them or challenging them, depending on the situation.

✓ Any intervention should occur as early as possible, such as at a project design stage. If introduced later, meaningful discussion will be constrained by budgets and time, and the facilitator's role may become tokenistic, technically unsound and unethical. Even if facilitation takes place later on, we must seek assurance from the implementers that major changes will be reflected in policy, methodology, budgeting and time line.

✓ Where change is planned at community level, we may need to help the organisation monitor its internal gender climate as well as community changes, keeping in mind that local perspectives to gender often differ from the way gender issues are interpreted at international level. We can help participants understand that what is good for their beneficiary community is also good for them and have found Naila Kabeer's tool useful in this respect (see Box 4.16, this volume).

✓ Gender biases are deeply rooted: addressing them shakes up values and culture. Using everyday life examples from home and using much humour will help loosen potential resistance. Making reference to a supportive legal system and approaching gender concerns from a human rights perspective can also help.

---

addressing staff beliefs on gender issues. As the others participants failed to respond, the facilitator had to take the lead: '*If your daughter came home severely beaten, what would you do?*' which generated a number of answers to provoke debate.

BUILDING THE PME CAPACITY OF BENEFICIARY GROUPS

An important dimension of sustainable development is the growth of 'beneficiary' organisations, with strong PME and capacity for learning (see Box 6.9). Development organisations therefore often aim to improve the PME capacity of community organisations (this also helps in their 'exit strategy'), although this aspect of PME is often confusingly brought under the banner of 'participatory PME',

Box 6.9 Community and NGO PME Systems in Coexistence

The Centre de Services aux Coopératives (CSC), à Rwandese NGO, identified sunflower growing as a sustainable enterprise for small farmers, whom it supported to form an association to access the required inputs and markets.

While CSC and the sunflower association share the long-term goals of improved living conditions and sustained community livelihoods, their short-term objectives are different: CSC wants to set up a vibrant association, with a leading market position, strong contacts with traders and fair pricing. To this end, CSC has offered training and its interests include relevance and effectiveness in strengthening the association. These objectives inform the selection of indicators and CSC staff carries prime responsibility for this data collection and analysis, though they involve the farmers for evaluation and to enrich their knowledge. This helps them gauge when the group has reached the stage where CSC support is no longer needed.

The sunflower association undertakes its own activities, such as taking care of input supply, developing its business relations, learning about the market and controlling the quality of its members' crop. They select their own indicators and make their M&E plan, for which they are responsible. They may ask CSC for advice, but it is their system, which is less formal than CSC's.

which we have earlier discussed (Chapter 5, section titled 'Learning and Beneficiary Participation in PME').

We have found that such efforts must rest on a sound analysis of learning taking place at the community level. Many communities and their organisations monitor and evaluate their work informally: they are effective learners for reasons of sheer survival. As facilitators, we then need to ask ourselves whether more formal PME systems are needed, or are superfluous. The answer might well depend on the role of the organisation concerned. Is it a village committee tackling wider development and governance issues for the entire community? Is it a women's savings club? A water users' association for farmers with access to irrigation? Or a producers' group, growing vegetables for the export market? All such groups may still continue to learn informally, but the extent of their connection with the external world (government, bank, irrigation department, traders) will compel them to formalise parts of their M&E, as partners in wider groupings.

As facilitators, we should, however, emphasise that the PME system of a beneficiary group should not replicate that of any NGO giving it support. We often find that an NGO that played a role in the formation of a beneficiary organisation continues to determine its agenda: this may be because of rigid project targets, a lack of confidence in the capacity of beneficiaries to do their own PME, an imposition of one's dream on the group, or impatience in allowing it to learn from its mistakes. The group's own PME system, formal or not, is then neglected, either because of the attitudes of formally educated development workers, or because they lack skills to facilitate the growth of the group's own PME and to determine when it is able to use PME independently, thus allowing the NGO to phase out its support.

Our role as PME facilitators is then to work with the NGO so that it identifies any such skills gap and develops its competence through demonstration, training and guided practice. This might include helping the NGO forge a more empowering approach, to clarify the roles of the 'doers' (community) and the 'facilitators' (NGO) and the *do's* and *don'ts* of such a facilitating role (see Box 6.10).

Box 6.10 Participatory PME Within and Without: Purvanchal Gramin Chetna Samiti in India

With a clear commitment to the participation of its beneficiaries in PME, Purvanchal Gramin Chetna Samiti (PGCS) in India has been assisted by PME facilitators to devise and institutionalise means to ensure this.

Beneficiary participation takes place at two levels. First, at the project level, where a PGCS project management committee is involved in any project planning and has both community and staff representation. The committee works with the staff to collect data; it examines monitoring reports from the field and takes necessary decisions.

Second is the PME of partner organisations: PGCS works through small self-help groups focusing on savings and credit and larger community organisations addressing social issues and carrying rights-based action. PGCS facilitates each of these to have their short- and long-term plans. PGCS staff have nurtured the skill to play a facilitator's role, avoiding any decision on behalf of the people.

This was not easy to achieve, given the initial tendency by staff to instruct rather than facilitate, justified by arguing that, as community members themselves, they were entitled to participate equally. Skills and attitudes needed to change: the facilitators conducted customised training on facilitation skills and participatory monitoring, which explained the perspective and elicited 'do's' and 'don'ts' from feedback during practical field sessions. PGCS has also introduced self-assessment tools to help the groups monitor their functioning and results.

THE NGO SECTOR HAS ITS CULTURE TOO

The collective culture of NGOs must also feature in our discussion of contextual issues, since NGOs display common characteristics that have much influence on their PME practice, their capacity to learn and thus on the facilitation process. One such characteristic is a tendency to display a measure of superiority, often implicitly justified by high-sounding mission statements, which usually refer to promoting the livelihoods, or defending the rights and interests, of marginalised people. Where they 'use' such worthy intentions, NGOs can develop a blaming culture, as when they look for external factors, rather than their own deficiencies, to justify programme results that are hard to find, or demand accountability from governments, when their own practices fall short of the standards they expect from others.

This attitude may also reflect another reality: NGOs increasingly have to compete for attention to secure funding. Competition can be positive, but can also result in difficult inter-NGO collaboration and foster a 'stripes on the shoulder' behaviour, for instance, in having a gender policy, a strategic plan, or up-to-date technology. 'Stripes' can be useful, but they can also be superficial, as when a strategic planning exercise is undertaken by an external consultant and is not internally owned. Stripes can also take the form of a 'performance first, learning later' approach and promote a culture of watching the neighbour. Paradoxically, many good results may be produced, but not be appreciated internally, especially when they do not comply with externally imposed concepts and tools.

A reluctance to share can take other forms: we thus find development organisations involved in similar programmes become inward-looking, arguing that the location, or nature, of 'their' beneficiary group is so specific that tailor-made solutions must be designed on the spot. Such claims to uniqueness then justify an almost unconscious defence mechanism against criticism and a feeling that there is little to learn from elsewhere, given one's superb track record.

The voluntary sector is also in many places changing its identity, such as where NGOs adopt a government, or private sector, culture and assume their ethics—good and bad. Opportunistic tendencies, the search for profile, contracts and donor funding can result in a loss of focus, with NGOs swinging back and forth between specialisation and integration, finding it difficult to balance meeting community needs with their own competencies and ambitions. A fuzzy identity and a disconnect between what the NGO professes to be and what it actually does can ensue, threatening organisational values in the process (see Box 6.11).

In spite of these challenges, we, of course, also recognise that many development organisations are committed to strict ethical practice, in terms of participation, transparency and equity, and are often innovative in their fields.

Box 6.11 Subcontracting and the Risk of Losing One's Focus

In Ghana, many health delivery organisations have responded positively to subcontracting opportunities, but there is a risk of loosing one's original vision/mission when doing so.

The initial problem analysis of many of these organisations emphasised deficiencies in healthcare, such as limited access for marginalised groups, especially women, or neglect of new diseases. Once subcontracted, however, these dimensions tend to recede in the NGOs' work. Although they may still adhere to principles of participation, equity, sustainability and prevention instead of cure, in practice they provide the same services as the government health institutions. A role play with the health staff in the NGO sector helped them to acknowledge this during a recent workshop.

What are the implications of this context for PME facilitation? The first is to make every effort to include this cultural dimension when planning a PME process. Organisations often 'live' this context, without clearly appreciating its consequences and even consciously, or unconsciously, negating some elements of it. Organisations should be helped to recognise these cultural issues: honesty and openness from the facilitator is appreciated, once a good rapport has been established.

Second, the effects of the sector's culture for the individuals we work with when supporting PME processes need to be kept constantly in mind (see Box 6.12). Thus, competitive pressures may lead to a fear of admitting mistakes and learning from them. It is also important to remember that the educational background of many NGO staff can hamper the 'improving' dimension of M&E as they often feel the need for scientific scope and are not easily convinced that a lighter approach can at times satisfy their information needs. In other cases, fears can reflect a lack of transparency, a real or imagined threat of losing one's job and of being watched by the bosses, all with clear consequences for PME systems and processes.

THE CHALLENGE OF DONOR RELATIONSHIPS

DONOR REQUIREMENTS

Donors range from small citizens' solidarity groups to governments and multilateral organisations, with different motives for making grants and various interests in PME systems. In terms of reporting, for instance, while the solidarity group may merely want to know if the funds have arrived in the recipient's bank account, the large donor may attach instructions to a contract and may request information to 'educate' the donor public. Reconciling these often fixed requirements with its own PME needs can be a challenge for the grant-receiving organisation. While some donors are sensitive to their partners' accountability and learning needs, others are only concerned with their own information requirements for project assessment, or expenditure control. In between, many variants exist.

Where donors insist on reporting formats and other requirements (and these may frequently change), this causes frustration and increases the workload, especially where an organisation has multiple donors with conflicting demands. Although such peculiarities can be cosmetic, successful initiatives in harmonising guidelines that take the recipient organisation's PME as the basis for project formulation and for reporting are rare. Because of the power relations at play, where a large part of the budget depends on donors, it is difficult to say 'no' to conditions and PME is often narrowly perceived as 'reporting' because it is defined by this relationship, rather than from a broader perspective of public accountability. Unless a good relationship with donors exists already, if reporting is seen as a form of control, recipients hesitate to disclose problems they confront and M&E may then lack transparency and undermine learning.

PME is also subject to fashion and trends, with 'development academics' and consultants often generating new ideas and approaches, usually when current practice fails to yield expected results (see also Box 1.1). These ideas often flow along an 'aid chain' linking development actors (individuals and organisations), in the development process. At one end, we find tax payers in the richer countries, donors and donor governments; these interact with international and national development organisations which, further along the chain, relate with community organisations and, finally the 'beneficiaries'. Along this chain, we can distinguish a flow of funds, ideas and conditions from North to South and, going in the other direction, an accountability and learning flow. The roles of the different actors evolve, as when tax payers now physically check on projects they contributed to, or even provide direct support to the target group, as with the recent tsunami disaster in East Asia.

The millennium development goals (MDGs) offer an example of the global harnessing of development ideas, and development organisations have come under pressure to reflect these in their PME system. Further, many countries have developed poverty reduction strategy papers (PRSPs), with MDGs as important targets: civil society organisations occasionally take part in the formulation of the PRSPs and may commit themselves to working on achieving MDGs. Where these organisations have not participated in such processes, they can still be indirectly influenced and required to report on MDGs, which may demand additional capacity from the planning stage.

Recent research on funding flows (see Further Reading) shows that, where donor funding is important, donor conditions are rarely experienced positively by local development actors. Donor conditions may relate to political circumstances (with funding on hold for several months at elections time, for instance), to the roles to be played by civil society programmes in poverty reduction, to programme content (service delivery, rights-based approaches, etc.) and to project design and implementation (tools for managing the project cycle, especially logframes), in addition to funding modalities and accountability systems. Actors in the chain then often impose PME requirements and formats to the next actors down the line, sometimes making them stricter in the process. Beyond these conditions, what we may call the international aid industry promotes a vision of change as essentially linear, predictable and controllable that is reflected in approaches and tensions with regard to PME (see Chapter 2, section titled 'Implications for Facilitators'). This results in increasing pressure on PME systems at all levels, which can lead to a clash with the local culture and can make organisations in the South donor- (rather than beneficiary-) oriented, unless negotiation skills can be enhanced.

NEGOTIATING WITH DONORS

If development organisations are often in awe of donors, dis-empowerment is not inescapable. First, there is rarely one single aid chain, but a network of them. Among larger development organisations in the South, a diversified funding base and respect for a successful track record contribute to a more balanced playing field when negotiating with donors. An organisation can also respond to demands in different ways: although some donors may be inflexible when it comes to reporting, it is worthwhile to negotiate to adapt at least parts of the reporting formats to fit the recipient's PME system. Where possible, donor representatives can be consulted at the design stage, taking care not to undermine autonomy. A knowledgeable insider can be approached to understand motives and dynamics and thus help the organisation in presenting its information. Although, when asked to harmonise their requirements with others, funders frequently mention their own 'back' donors' inflexibility, it can be worthwhile to persuade them to try and influence them. Demands may not always be as tough as they appear at first sight and, while not all donors are flexible, such efforts are rarely a total waste of time. Even among smaller organisations, there have been successes in negotiating planning and reporting procedures that reflect their needs. A few funders, or more commonly individuals within donor agencies, are also increasingly open to more flexible working methods. This can be enhanced by face-to-face discussions, the provision of appropriate training, negotiations beginning right at the start of the project planning stage and joint evaluations.

Negotiations can aim at different outcomes. The best of these for the recipient organisation is its donors' wholesale acceptance of its PME system and reporting formats (assuming that they are adequate for accountability and learning purposes). This requires an analysis of the recipient's PME system and reports, of the donor's requirements, and negotiating over any differences. This makes no additional demand for information gathering and presentation. Moreover, reporting follows the approach of the organisation engaged in the development initiative and thus enhances accountability and learning at that level.

The second best option is to ask the donors involved to harmonise their requirements into a single format and system. This may be based on the format used by one of them, preferably the format that suits the recipient best. A third option, should the previous two not yield results, requires the recipient to develop a PME system to meet its own requirements at the outset. In all likelihood, most donor requirements will also be met but, where this is not the case, further requirements can be dealt with by a series of add-ons, which is preferable to having donor requirements as the starting point.

We share here an example of NGOs that achieved positive results in negotiations with donors on their PME practice (see Box 6.13). This led to more independence in managing their own affairs towards the higher objectives that they had set for themselves, beyond the project level. The example shows that dependence on funds does not necessarily mean acceptance of all conditions and that a recipient can retain a total organisation approach. Donors often impose strict regulations out of apprehension, usually because they feel the need to demonstrate their control over the funds provided. When the development organisation does not offer its own clear way forward, the donor easily prescribes contents and procedures. Thus, at a recent workshop with donor agencies, bishops and managers working for Ghanaian church-based

Box 6.13 More Autonomy from Donors through Effective Communication and Proactive PME Practice

A partner NGO in the Philippines recently developed a new project. This, as well as its organisational objectives and contextual and strategic analysis, was discussed with their donor step-by-step.

When it came to contract negotiations, the NGO ensured that it was not the donor who prescribed the budget headings for the project in the first place. It took care to inform the donor of its financial and information system, with a focus on M&E beyond the project level. The structure of the project budget was agreed, in accordance with the NGO's existing overall system. The donor was impressed with its partner's proactive and systematic approach and found it easy to consent, only adding a few specific demands to meet its own information needs.

The NGO later went a step further and requested flexibility from the donor to agree to budget amendments during the project period. Previously, a report explaining the difference between budgeted and actual costs was required. The NGO explained that they would report clear M&E outcomes to justify any decision to alter a budget, arguing that it was better to plan flexibly and adjust costs to achieve objectives than to remain within an original budget when systematic monitoring highlighted a flaw that compromised results. Two procedures were considered: (a) changing the budget composition, that is, more funds would be spent for some activities and less on others, or (b) in addition to the above, increasing the total budget. The first scenario was accepted on the basis of proficient M&E reports, while specific agreement would be sought from the donor for the second scenario.

Experience was built with this approach, which became known as 'the latest estimate' concept. Other partner NGOs learned much from it and over time used it to improve their PME system. Procedure (a) was appreciated as a flexible and helpful approach, matching appropriate authority with appropriate responsibility, but little headway was made with procedure (b), given donors' reluctance to commit additional funds.

organisations, all parties in this particular aid chain agreed that a PME system accommodating performance measurement is needed and that partner organisations are well placed to reassure donors by means of clear result statements.

Looking beyond our partner organisations, it is thus important to consider the mind shifts needed at the donor level. A clearer, more consistent donor approach to PME is essential and, insofar as we, PME facilitators, or desk officers in donor agencies, have the

Box 6.14 PME and the 'Aid Chain'

✓ Explaining how a development organisation is usually part of an aid chain can act as a powerful stimulant to understand PME constraints and opportunities and the need to negotiate conditions with other actors in the chain, including partner communities. As a facilitator describes, 'I start explaining the result chain by asking participants what makes them proud in implementing their projects. They usually respond with positive results in the community. This makes up the first part of the results chain, linking NGOs with communities. Without achieving these results, staff would gradually loose interests. I then add the next actor, the donor agency, and ask them the same question, about what they think motivates the desk officer to continue funding NGOs. The same answer pertains: it is about information on positive changes: results again. The story continues with the tax payer, explaining the role of the person with voting power, advocating for international collaboration, or deciding to directly sponsor a project. This explanation helps to better understand the connections between the various actors in the chain, their own crucial role in it and how to become more proactive.'

✓ The fact that donors depend on development organisations for results and their survival within this chain, can highlight interdependence, as well as the need for a development organisation to produce results that convince other actors in this chain of their quality of work.

✓ Sharing examples of successful negotiations with donors and encouraging donor diversity can help build self-confidence in handling these power relationships.

✓ To avoid the perception of a facilitator as a 'donor-by-proxy', we can encourage the local organisation to contract the facilitator, or, better, to initiate any request for PME support itself.

✓ We can play a legitimate role in engaging the donors too: have they reflected on their own key information needs? Do they promote learning within their organisation? To what extent do they involve partner organisations in developing PME practices and formats?

opportunity, we should influence practice at that end of the chain, while increasing partner organisations' capacity and supporting their negotiating skills for effective PME practice (see Box 6.14).

RELATING WITH OTHER STAKEHOLDERS AND INFLUENCES

THE REGULATORY ENVIRONMENT

Regulations prevailing in a particular context often set minimum standards that affect PME practice, which registered organisations have to comply with. These include:

1. **Government procedures and reporting formats:** In some countries, the government only requires that an activity, or organisation, be registered. In others, approval procedures are extensive and reports on activities, or results are demanded. This is often the case for strictly regulated sectors, including healthcare, education and infrastructure, where activities must adhere to official standards and regularly be reported on. These requirements normally have to be integrated in the project, or organisational, PME system, the necessary resources allocated and data gathered to ensure formal acceptance of plans and activities. Such regulations may also have implications for project implementation, such as hiring of personnel, or the use of educational material. The government must be contacted to establish the implications these standards, including integrating and reporting on MDGs, may have for the organisation, its activities and its reports. As noted earlier, however, an unquestioning adherence to standards and procedures can constrain learning and promote a reactive behaviour, although some NGOs have successfully influenced policy frameworks, including PRSPs. Some development organisations might also wish to use the prescribed system, while adding information relevant to their own purpose, for example, by showing the effects of an educational programme for a particular group, or geographical area.

2. **Accounting requirements:** Official accounting regulations exist in most countries and will normally affect the design of the financial system of a development organisation. This usually requires contracting a certified auditing firm and providing financial

For NGOs in India, tax returns to government can be complex, often requiring a special exercise and sometimes outside assistance. Returns are therefore often inaccurate or late, attracting heavy fines. This was recently addressed by an Indian NGO, with the help of a consultant who facilitated the improvement of financial reporting to the government, including tax returns.

The consultant helped the NGO see that when its own reporting needs—and the financial systems based on this—were taken as a starting point, most government reporting requirements could be met, while any additional information needed could be built into the internal system. The same could be said and done for donor requirements.

Financial reporting to different stakeholders often benefits from not being handled as individual requirements, but as related to each other and deduced from one integrated system, whose starting point is the information needed to manage the organisation itself. Government and donor reporting can often largely be derived from this, the rest being added to meet specific needs.

information in a simple and timely fashion to all stakeholders (government, donors, etc.). This should be based, as much as possible, on the management needs of the organisation, although it may at times conflict with government reporting rules, as when the legislation classifies donated assets as not belonging to a charity, whereas for all intents and purposes they do. Nevertheless, we have found (see Box 6.15) that reporting requirements can be satisfied in a more efficient manner when they meet as much as possible the information needs of the development organisation first.

DATA, TECHNOLOGY AND PHYSICAL INFRASTRUCTURE

In many poor countries data is either absent, or scarce and unreliable. Statistical information may be inaccurate because of lack of resources to regularly collect and store it; it may also be inaccessible because of poor infrastructure, or because the more powerful do not want to disseminate it. Data may also be undifferentiated, with limited focus on, say, the poorer sections of the population. There may be geographical and other barriers too: large areas to cover, unsafe conditions, seasonal factors, or poor transport. The manipulation of figures for political purposes can also reduce their usefulness, emphasising the need for cautious use.

Where official data sources are imperfect, other databases can be created, usually for specific purposes. Baseline surveys on particular issues, usually in limited geographical areas, can serve as a basis for PME, although their use by others and their combination with varied sources of information can be problematic when definitions and methods are not comparable. This partly explains why organisations often collect new data for their PME systems, rather than use existing information.

Information technology also shapes PME systems, whose sophistication largely depends on whether an organisation has access to such technology. The formats for PME often assume the existence of computerised systems which, while often useful, may not be appropriate for smaller organisations, may focus on quantitative rather than qualitative data and may foster dependency on computerised resources to the detriment of participatory and locally-driven analysis. Very often too, formats are helpful in data collecting, more rarely to analyse it.

New means of electronic communications, such as the internet, or mobile phones and short text messaging, offer new PME avenues, as the Chorlavi example (see Box 6.16) shows. Information, including that of governments, is increasingly available on the internet and we can play a useful role as facilitators to encourage partners to make good use of this constantly improving resource.

Box 6.16 Technology and New Avenues for PME Learning

Chorlavi (www.grupochorlavi.org), an internet-facilitated development network, started in Ecuador in 1998 to share lessons on sustainable agriculture and rural development in Latin America.

The first years of the network were experimental: member organisations would send in proposals, in which learning assumed a central place, and Chorlavi would fund a few initiatives. Experience sharing on the web was also organised. With time, the project funding component grew, as well as web-based electronic conferences for sharing and discussions. The membership also increased, to the present 700 organisations, with an even larger outreach. The network is informal, with a strong activity (rather than structure) focus. A board supervises the learning processes and one organisation, Rimisp, manages Chorlavi as a programme.

There is a constant quest for learning. As members initially hesitated to use e-mail to express opinions, it was decided to meet physically once a year. Other obstacles included the quality of projects: how could the board arrive at a fair judgement of the eligibility of projects solely on paper? Second, certain regions and organisations were under-represented in this project circuit. Third, after a period without thematic focus, the network decided to adopt specific themes annually and invited other social actors to participate in their selection. To ensure a fair selection, a rigorous framework was designed, which is updated by systematic annual reflection.

Chorlavi has established internal M&E for its own accountability and developed a conceptual framework for this, with a constant search for improved performance through annual reviews. As sharing has been rather passive so far, the network now wants to focus on a multiplier effect of lessons learnt. Two concerns remain to be tackled: first, the emerging self-selection mechanism of such a web-based tool, where some organisations

(Box 6.16 Contd.)

(Box 6.16 Contd.)

are quick to participate in more abstract and policy-oriented discussions, while others, working at a more practical level, are difficult to reach. Second, Chorlavi has placed much emphasis on the project fund at the expense of other forms of systematising experiences and sharing.

From a facilitation point of view, one pillar of success has been the drive of the facilitator, the Rimisp director, whose reflective role was crucial throughout this growth period. He was also supported by desk officers within the funding agencies, who contributed to learning and reflection processes, but avoided dominating the agenda. The transparency and quality of communication, the flexibility and the learning dimension were also crucial. Learning has been systematic thanks to a small and transparent management structure that has proved responsive to the needs of a diverse audience, through ongoing evaluation. The Chorlavi experience also shows that it is possible to stimulate people and organisations to systematise their experiences in the field and to offer them on the web.

KNOWLEDGE AND BUSINESS ORGANISATIONS

Universities, other academic groups and consultants can play a supportive role in data analysis and in developing PME systems. As 'knowledge producers', they can participate in the design and testing of new systems, from which a development organisation can benefit. Forging relations with knowledge institutions can therefore contribute to the strengthening of PME.

Public–private partnerships have also become more prominent in development work. They connect the state and development organisations to the corporate sector, which has its own values and PME standards, including restrictions on sharing information that might undermine a competitive advantage. On the other hand, cooperation with civil society organisations is often seen as less threatening than with other firms, as they may not be competitors, and corporate giving is also increasingly part of this relationship (see Box 6.17).

**Box 6.17 Donor, Business and Smallholder Farmers
Working Together**

For the past three years, a Dutch funding agency has established partnerships with companies in four African countries to promote access to markets for small farmers. The focus is on contract farming, linking companies and farmers in a contractual arrangement, with the expectation that both parties benefit. The funding agency and companies have also agreed to a learning exercise, as they both lack experience of this type of arrangement. A facilitator coordinates this learning process with consultants to help in data collection and analysis.

The lessons learnt so far include the need for a shared vision on this model and what it is meant to achieve for the target groups. Second, one must acknowledge two different, but complementary, learning agenda: the companies focus on financial and economic data (even though they have a social interest), whereas the funding agency stresses socio-political aspects. The facilitator must bring these together while playing a proactive role to foster communication among partners who come from different cultures. Third, transparency is a condition for developing a strong contract farming model, with larger companies finding it easier to share their information with the other stakeholders. Finally, one must keep the research component as easy as possible, using simple baselines and frequent, rapid M&E studies, as this elicits wide participation (see also Box 4.14, this volume).

CONCLUSION: CONTEXT MONITORING

A development organisation usually works in a geographical area, or sector, where other actors and forces are active, all situated in a wider cultural context. It can share information and analysis with these actors, be a critical sparring partner, give advice, or support, or set up complementary programmes. Relationships may be collaborative, or competitive, but stakeholders surrounding an organisation will share an interest in its activities and influence its social acceptability, reputation and legitimacy.

We often find that the way a development organisation relates and positions itself in its operating environment determines success as much as what it directly does. One illustration of this importance is the proliferation of networks, coalitions and alliances of development actors we increasingly encounter on all continents, although we have seen that sharing and working with others is not always a straightforward matter. When development organisations enter collaborative mechanisms, new PME challenges emerge:

Box 6.18 Context Monitoring: Life-saving and Innovation-inducing in the Philippines ˮ

Tri-People Consortium for Peace, Progress and Development of Mindanao (TRICOM), a Philippino NGO, has been working with remote communities in Mindanao to support them in claiming their ancestral lands. Context monitoring is essential in these areas because war and disease can lead to radical changes. The isolation of these communities has provided an operating base and recruitment ground for armed anti-government groups.

After the TRICOM staff had built trust with communities more familiar with gun traders and suspicious of outsiders coming to steal their spirits and knowledge, they helped the elders in the sensitive process of documenting their hitherto oral history, for submission to government as evidence of their land claims.

Respect for indigenous beliefs not only ensured acceptance by the community, but also security of life for the staff. With the area constantly visited by armed groups, community leaders took responsibility for the programme team, giving information whenever armed groups were present and orienting the leaders of the armed group on the programme purpose. Monitoring the recurrent outbreaks of conflict and disease also led to new interventions, such as relief and emergency operations and a health initiative to combat malaria.

The programme team thus had to include diverse information in their monthly monitoring, including developments in the peace process between the government and the rebel groups; increase or decrease in military operations; political developments, rumours of a military coup affecting troop movements; as well as incidence of malaria.

Box 6.19 Context Monitoring

✓ Finding out as much as possible about the context of a partner organisation at the outset of a PME support process is essential. This should allow the facilitator to clarify whether support should focus on challenging, or managing contextual elements, bearing in mind that challenging contextual forces must be within the realm of the possible, especially for small organisations.

✓ Since context monitoring often happens informally, it may help to develop sharing and documenting mechanisms, such as making contextual indicators explicit. Similarly, it may help to examine the extent of staff information on any of the following, in addition to the reflection points (discussed in Chapter 3, section titled 'Beyond the Organisation and its Programmes') in their daily work:

  • Government sectoral policies and type of PME systems in use in ministries, or departments.
  • Donor policies, including shifts in themes, procedures and funding priorities.
  • Performance of other development organisations and bi/multilateral programmes; relevant best practices.
  • Strength and quality of collaboration with other actors.

✓ Helping partners reflect on contextual changes is also useful, since the environment in which they evolve is rarely static. The 'Manual of Project Cycle Management' (see Further Reading) can help organisations decide on the degree of importance of external factors, or assumptions, and whether they need monitoring.

✓ Where a logframe is used, a facilitator can make reference to the assumption column that contains many of these externalities, so that it is no longer informally monitored, but becomes the object of more systematic reflection, such as at staff meetings, or other regular events.

✓ Partner organisations often appreciate having a good understanding of the context of PME as well, such as the operations of the aid chain, the interdependence of different actors, and their linked information needs.

there is less direct control over initiatives, planning becomes complex; different actors may have their own M&E requirements; sharing information does not come easily, there may be a tendency to want to do everything oneself and downplay best practices in existence elsewhere within the sector.

We have also seen that managers frequently monitor contextual changes. This might include changes in government policy, new donor interests, the performance of other development organisations and the emergence of new ones. Such information is often collected informally, rarely documented, but routinely used for decision-making (see Box 6.18). A thorough examination of the context, with its many elements and patterns of distribution of power can indeed be complicated. Although such analysis may be hard for facilitators who are 'outsiders', this can also clarify aspects of the environment that are taken for granted by 'insiders'. Contextual analysis is where we can often help, if undertaken jointly with staff and other key stakeholders of the organisations we are working with (see Box 6.19).

PART 3
FURTHER
CUSTOMISING PME

7

EVERY ORGANISATION IS UNIQUE

Unsurprisingly, we have found that strengthening PME is more successful when customising our work to reflect the specificity of the partner organisation, including its external context. This chapter discusses four inter-linked organisational characteristics to keep in mind and shares our facilitation experiences. We review values and perspectives on change, organisational leadership, age and size, and type of organisation.

VALUES AND PERSPECTIVES ON CHANGE

Given our 'total organisation' perspective on PME, the most important characteristic of a partner organisation lies in its core values and vision/mission, which inform its analysis of poverty and powerlessness, and define the role it wants to play in society. We have argued that PME should help to monitor and evaluate whether this vision/mission is effectively being achieved. It is also essential for the facilitator to review the *nature* of the change an organisation is committed to in relation to its capacity and its problem analysis (which inform the mission/vision). We have

Box 7.1 Values, Change and PME Facilitation

We recently started a discussion on the values of an NGO in Niger in the context of PME facilitation. Established at a time when structural adjustment policies affected employment opportunities for young professionals, the NGO had increasingly acted as a subcontractor for programmes identified by donor agencies, via the national government. Of its three programmes, one—a food security initiative—had been identified by the NGO itself, with much popular participation. The other two were subcontracted and identified in a more top–down fashion.

Although our facilitation initially only focused on the food security programme, we later turned our attention to the other two. There was hesitance at first, but we insisted that even as a contractor, the NGO had an obligation and opportunity to learn about the effectiveness and efficiency of all its programmes, the relevance of the approach used and their contribution to its mission/vision.

Learning across programmes then becomes important. Staff and management responded positively, helped by the involvement of the same technical staff in all three programmes. We stressed that while there may be a sound strategic internal reason to implement diverse initiatives as part of a learning and experimental agenda, the external image created, including with donors, is a negative one. It is then the task of the facilitators to help the organisation put in place this strategic planning and learning process; to help it describe its strategic considerations in choosing to implement different types of programmes, some possibly not immediately in tune with its philosophy. Even when implementing a project as a contractor, for instance, a change agenda might include influencing the opinion and attitude of government officials, or donor agencies, which will then need monitoring.

Facilitating such learning at the vision/mission level can help in two ways: first, to discuss internal coherence and to make informal learning more explicit. This can help reconcile long-term vision/mission for the target group with any short-term internal objective the organisation may have, such as protecting its employees. Second, it is essential for external communication, especially with donors, to emphasise this change agenda. Neglecting it makes organisations vulnerable funding-wise, as donors then fail to see the strategic rationale for implementing diverse programmes.

found that such considerations are often undermined by pressing implementation issues, or by vague problem analysis, hindering subsequent scrutiny and reflection, or an analysis at the national level, whereas the intervention is local.

The nature of the change sought may entail a transformative role (effecting a social change), or a consolidating one (offering a service to meet a structural need in society). It may also stress a social function versus an economic one. This role, and the perspective on change it implies, can evolve: many NGOs, for instance, start life with a transformative agenda, but move on to traditional social services delivery. Others may move towards a more economic role, such as micro-finance, or business development services. Yet others specialise in generating information and knowledge, engaging in policy development, or sector-wide research and may in the process develop into partially profit-driven enterprises, as some clients readily pay for their products. We have observed organisations struggle with following their vision on change when involved in subcontracting (see Box 7.1 and Boxes 5.2 and 7.14). A concern for participation and access for specific groups may then disappear, as the change agenda becomes more externally driven, rather than reflecting internal beliefs and values. The PME facilitation process must tackle such fundamental organisational orientations, holding a mirror to the organisation, so that it becomes aware of any inconsistencies, or at least the inconsistencies it projects to its external stakeholders (see Box 7.2).

Box 7.2 Facilitating Reflection on Values and Perspectives on Change

✓ Remaining open as facilitators and striving to understand our partners' perspectives on change is important, as our point of view may not always be in tune with local analysis and values.

✓ We have found it useful to take every opportunity to help examine how the mission/vision is translated into operational plans and vice-versa.

✓ Participatory methods to illustrate potential tensions between values and operations can help participants adopt a multi-focus perspective on themselves. Such methods include role plays and the red hat ('be critical, think of constraints'), green hat ('think positively, of solutions'), yellow hat ('think local, be realistic'), blue hat ('think global, be visionary') method.

ORGANISATIONAL LEADERSHIP AND PARTICIPATION

The type of leadership is another important aspect that informs the success of PME facilitation, in addition to staff skills and attitudes, which we have reviewed earlier. Thus, a laid-back leader may shy away from a decision to introduce effective PME, or to act upon PME findings, at best focusing on cosmetic, or popular options. PME practice can also be affected by a domineering, or aggressive, leadership, where staff are intimidated, or snubbed, by a leader too quick to conclude and decide, without allowing collective reflection. In such a situation, however good the PME system may be in theory, it will be difficult to implement and the facilitator will have to bring this to the leaders' attention.

The leaders' objectivity, especially when drawing learning points, will also determine the effectiveness of PME, particularly M&E. Objectivity is essential to analyse achievements (or their lack thereof) and the reasons for these, as well as strengths and weaknesses in the various dimensions of the organisation. Otherwise, justifying rather than understanding will keep the organisation in its own world, in the false and comfortable perception that it is performing at its best. The facilitator will in such a situation have to provoke further reflection, for instance, by presenting similar examples from other organisations.

We have also observed the importance of leadership in skills development. In the examples discussed in Box 7.3, the leadership had to express its trust in the ability of the field staff, who were encouraged to experiment with a new PME approach. Though

Box 7.3 Ignore the Leadership at Your Peril!

In a recent capacity-building process in eastern India, all 25 field staff of a grass-roots NGO were trained in micro-planning skills. This was to enhance a facilitative approach to allow partner communities prepare their own plans and foster their sense of ownership. The staff showed appreciation of the new approach, recognising their earlier deficiencies and enthusiastically practised the new skills.

Four months on, monitoring indicated that the new approach had not been applied. The senior staff had not recognised the need for micro-planning as much as their field colleagues and had directed them to focus on other tasks. The PME facilitators had to organise a refresher training attended by the NGO leadership: once it was convinced, the new approach took root in the organisation.

The necessity to involve the leadership in PME processes had become starkly apparent, as a second example, this time from Bangladesh, also illustrates. Working with a large national organisation with a staff of 900, good results have been obtained and the organisation is well on its way to incorporating micro-planning and facilitative styles because of the commitment of the leadership. Training involved a group of 30 middle-level staff and led to an elaborate plan to train all field staff in-house. External consultants were also invited to carry out a short orientation programme for the top leaders to help them adopt facilitative styles not only in project work, but also within the organisation.

Box 7.4 Involving the Leadership

✓ We have found it essential to ensure that there is a clear commitment by the leadership (board and management) when planning a PME capacity-building process. Eliciting commitment across the organisation on the practice of PME must then follow, by facilitating the development of norms to be followed and, later, by providing follow-up and feedback on the organisation's ability to put new concepts and systems into practice.

✓ Where necessary, personal sessions with the leaders can emphasise the advantages of creating a climate fostering dialogue and free expression. This can include exposure to best practices, against which the leaders can be challenged and become more objective.

✓ We can suggest external M&E professionals to provide objective feedback to the organisation. While external evaluations have long been common practice, hiring external persons to monitor programmes throughout their execution, as well as other organisational dimensions, is increasing.

aware of limitations, the leadership allowed staff to make mistakes, learn from them and develop new skills in the process.

FACILITATION OF PME AND ORGANISATIONAL GROWTH

The age and size of a partner organisation (or its position in a life-cycle) will also need to inform customised PME facilitation. As an organisation moves from birth to pioneering stage, to mid-size and, possibly, later becomes larger and more mature, PME facilitation needs will change and have to reflect transition challenges. This section highlights our experiences in dealing with development organisations at different stages of growth and as they move from one to the next.

PIONEERING ORGANISATIONS

In pioneering organisations, which are often quite small in size and scale of work, there is much preoccupation with identifying the activities required to meet the mission/vision. A young organisation will often depend on informal, oral, sometimes unstructured processes. Hierarchy is largely absent, exchanges of views are likely to be frank, and planning collective. Similarly, monitoring may well be participatory and self-critical. At this stage, PME tends to focus on ensuring the relevance of activities. Operational planning may predominate, with limited long-term, strategic planning. The relevance of any output may be unclear as the focus is on achieving *adequate* output. There is likely to be more 'spiritual' thought, less 'systems' thinking and limited drive for efficiency/effectiveness. In financial terms, the organisation may have a basic accounting, budgeting and M&E system.

Our experiences suggest that such organisations often find PME issues hard to assimilate as they are perceived as complicated, even superfluous. The facilitator then has to focus on conceptual clarity, discuss the purpose and principles of PME and bring leaders and staff to a consensus. At times, younger organisations are also unnecessarily critical of their own practices and systems. We can remind our partners that 'well begun is half done' and take care to acknowledge good practices to strengthen their confidence. Established customs, such as discussing the views of team members and making critical comments on their work, are valuable, and space should be provided to bring these onto an official agenda. Multi-tasking is also beneficial and we have not found it to lead to confused staff, as often feared. Finally, the need to remain flexible, to review and upgrade practices needs to be emphasised, in contrast to crushing spontaneity and introducing heavy systems and practices. While some data-based planning and monitoring can be initiated at this stage, a step-by-step approach, moving from the simple to the complex, is more appropriate.

To foster organisational growth and sustainability, we must also bring home the message that being strategic in decision-making is essential right from the outset. This entails looking at the total organisation from the beginning, avoiding any perception that, being small, a focus on projects is sufficient. This includes periodically reviewing and clarifying the partner's role in the development sector, its philosophy and approach. It also requires highlighting the importance of clear decisions on such issues as target group, geographical spread, type of staffing, community participation strategy, norms for accountability and transparency, even donor selection, to ensure complementarity in values and approaches. In addition, M&E, which is initially mostly informal and is directed at outputs, can help focus on the relevance of activities to contribute to the mission. In financial terms, facilitation may concentrate on helping to develop PME systems where accounting becomes more activity-based and where budgeting moves from being only a planning tool to becoming a management tool for cost control (see Box 7.5).

Box 7.5 Facilitating PME Processes in a Pioneer Organisation
✓ A good start is to agree on PME rationale and principles and to build on existing PME practice, bringing the informal to the surface, stressing flexibility and a step-by-step approach to avoid unnecessary complexities.
✓ We can also usefully verify the intervention logic to ensure focus, with activities contributing to the mission, avoiding over-diversification and being overambitious. This is part of looking at the total organisation, thinking strategically and clarifying organisational values and development approach from the outset.
✓ Strengthening self-confidence is often necessary. This can be done by creating spaces to openly discuss any uncertainties. The proximity of beneficiaries can offer an opportunity to check assumptions.
✓ We can facilitate the development of financial systems towards activity-based accounting and task-setting budgeting (see Chapter 4, this volume, section on 'Inspired Budgeting').

MID-SIZE ORGANISATIONS

Growth brings its set of complexities and opportunities. As programmes diversify, new staff with different backgrounds, skills and perspectives join the organisation. Hierarchy sets in and, with more projects, come more donors, with whom communication must be maintained.

This growth calls for a change in the nature of PME. The all-inclusive, informal style is no longer practical in all situations.

The sense of belonging may vary across the organisation and a tension between new and old staff, between 'barefoot' and 'qualified' professionals develops. As managers get drawn away from field work, the need for a management information system emerges and programme quality becomes an issue, with tension also emerging between 'growth' and 'participation' objectives. At this stage, PME systems mix the formal and informal, oral and written. The organisation tries to introduce systems and practices, often without PME facilitators. Donors will have drawn attention to PME, sometimes resulting in diverse systems, with varying degrees of sophistication, or overlaps, promoted by different consultants.

Mid-size organisations are often caught up in a whirlpool of change and exposed to ideas from various quarters. Staff tend to be quickly upset by criticisms of their PME practices. The PME facilitator will therefore first have to understand existing systems and practices well, carefully avoiding any assumption that there is only void, chaos, or no previous history. We have also found it worthwhile to spend time before facilitation to study culture and perceptions on the purpose of PME. The task is to build on what exists and to foster staff confidence by acknowledging good practice and working out how it can be incorporated in any revised structure, or procedure. It is equally important to help the organisation and its various stakeholders identify ongoing problems, their causes and remedies, avoiding a situation where the organisation merely adds new practices to old ones, thus creating unnecessary work. The process of PME facilitation must allow for comparison of the old and the new and for developing a clear way forward.

Structural issues—vertical and horizontal relationships—will also need attention, especially where past decisions have led to confusion. Rationalisation of the work culture, with increasing bureaucracy, might have undermined some of the idealism the organisation started with. The facilitator will need to ensure clarity on these issues and, in particular, help middle managers see the organisation as a whole, rather than in terms of 'their' projects only. Staff will need motivating to accept more direct responsibilities for quality results with increased focus on effects and impact, as pressure for performance builds up. With growth, a clash of different project approaches can emerge, with inconsistencies in planning and monitoring, allowing best and worst practices to coexist. A poor fit with the organisation's values and overall approach, duplication of target group and of services delivered and overlapping reporting requirements are issues that may then require attention. If there is more than one donor and exposure to several consultants, establishing links and similarities, and building the capacity of the organisation to deal with a variety of approaches and reporting formats may also be needed.

For financial PME, facilitation may need to focus on how monitoring can produce relevant management information. This will involve more objective-oriented operational and strategic planning, with attention to cost-efficiency. With the budget-holder accepting accountability for agreed targets, budgeting should become future- and task-oriented. Accounting will thus have to move beyond bookkeeping and include accounting policies and internal controls, with basic cost allocation to activities, including all overheads, eventually allowing reporting and evaluation to start integrating their narrative and financial dimensions. Cost-efficiency and cost-effectiveness should become important evaluation elements.

As we address these issues, facilitating internal learning and building on good existing internal practices will lead to refinement of systems, plans and consistency of approach, keeping staff capacity in mind. There is no need to be perfect right from the start, but facilitating mid-size organisations takes time not only because of

Box 7.6 Facilitating PME Processes in a Mid-size Organisation
✓ A good understanding of existing PME systems and culture, however rudimentary, is a useful starting point.
✓ By building on the existing, acknowledging good practices and pointing out deficiencies, we can tackle PME in relation to the emerging complexity of the organisational structure.
✓ Fostering a total organisational approach to PME and a vision that goes beyond particular projects will help identify inconsistencies and duplication between project approaches. Helping with a systemic integration of financial PME aspects can be part of this.
✓ Promoting more systematic effect and impact M&E, as part of facilitating internal learning processes, is often important in mid-sized organisations.

what needs to be learnt, but also what needs to be unlearnt. It is for this reason that we need to agree on an entire PME process from the very beginning (see Box 7.6).

MATURE/LARGE ORGANISATIONS

These organisations have moved on in scale and diversity, the leaders are more involved in management functions and specialised departments for human resources, fundraising and the like may have emerged. The PME functions are likely to have been given serious thought and a PME department may have been created, then closed and reopened with a different role: that of PME facilitation, rather than planning and monitoring. A mature hierarchy may conflict with participatory PME. Management information systems, in such organisations, become complex, but do not necessarily lead to appropriate and timely decision-making. Although a larger size may bring larger budgets and access to specialists, some organisations may grow to have offices in more than one location, thus posing further challenges for effective PME. During this phase, pitfalls include too much information, limited activity, weariness of change and ineffective coordination. Large organisations can suffer from an overemphasis on systems and procedures, at the expense of a culture of learning and reflecting on their mission/vision. People resort to filling in reports and adhering to deadlines, but may only reflect critically on their work in informal spaces, leading to negative feelings rather than useful change in the organisation. In contrast with the lack of confidence that characterises many younger organisations, we can encounter a 'we-know-it-all' attitude and a feeling that too much change is not feasible. The litmus test lies in whether such an organisation becomes bureaucratic and 'stuck', or whether it manages to develop systems that ensure adherence to its original vision and values and promote learning throughout its structure (see Box 7.7).

In such a context, the facilitator will need to critically analyse and effectively contribute to the development of PME practice. There is no need to engage in PME basics. Dealing with such organisations requires knowledge, skills as well as the right attitude, without any bias of the 'large is bad' kind.

Box 7.7 Size, Hierarchy and PME Practice

A large organisation in Bangladesh benefited from a good system of data collection on key performance indicators. This data was progressively compiled and sent on to the next level in the organisation. Analysis and subsequent decisions were, however, entirely in the hands of the top management. The field workers, who were primarily responsible for data collection, therefore largely perceived their input as alien. A project monitoring unit brought the analysis to the management and often made presentations before the regional staff, challenging them in areas of poor performance. The project monitoring unit was seen as a monitor and evaluator by the implementing staff, much to the dislike of the project monitoring unit personnel.

Facilitators then helped to streamline the planning and monitoring functions of the organisation. One task was to redefine the role of the project monitoring unit into a facilitator rather than a monitor and to include planning in its remit. Another was to ensure that each level in the organisation analysed data, took decisions that were within its purview and made suggestions where it could not make decisions. This increased the field workers' sense of purpose in data collection.

Given the size of the organisation, the facilitators had to develop a step-by-step process. One of the challenges has been to bring the implementers away from any tendency to blame 'the conditions', the government, or the community, for the lack of results, and to look internally to improve staff capacity, discipline, systems and work methods.

One of our tasks may be to institutionalise PME practice across the organisation. This could include supporting any existing PME units, or departments, to clarify their role, so that they enhance the quality of PME and engage the different stakeholders, rather then alienate programme staff from PME, a danger if the terms of reference of such a department are not carefully drawn. Another concern is the role of various management levels in PME, with a risk of PME becoming a central function. Our facilitating challenge will then be to help ensure that it remains decentralised, where collection of information at the 'grass-roots' is followed by its compilation and analysis, even decision-making to the extent possible, at that very level. We may also need to consider, with the leadership, what channels exist–and should exist–for gathering ideas, views and decisions from all stakeholders and thus help the organisation better reflect on its learning processes, as the management of change, teamwork and networking with other actors become more prominent. The organisation may thus need help in becoming more self-regulating and more relationship-oriented.

With regard to financial PME, clear links are required between all levels of planning, from the strategic level to the organisational and operational levels, leading to a fully integrated system. Accounting must respond to financial management demands, with bookkeepers and management accountants reporting to a financial manager. Finance staff may need to be better recognised, including their remuneration. At this stage, budgeting must be participatory and learning oriented, bringing finance and programme staff together with sufficient understanding of each other's fields. Monitoring, reporting and evaluation will need to reflect unity of purpose, increased organisational impact and staff motivation to learn collectively and initiate change.

Box 7.8 Facilitating PME Processes in More Mature Organisations

✓ We should only consider working with such an organisation if our PME experience is sufficient to contribute to the development of complex systems (including finance) and if we recognise that 'big' is not necessarily bad, although simplification might often be called for. We must also recognise that large organisations need time to change and therefore require patience to enlist wide ownership and leadership commitment.

✓ If a separate PME department is in existence, or is to be established, a likely facilitation focus is to ensure that other staff are not alienated from PME, such as by decentralising decision-making responsibilities.

✓ We may need to foster learning and reflection mechanisms, especially where the focus is too 'hardware-oriented'. Refocusing on the mission might also be necessary where it has become a distant concept.

✓ A focus on collaboration, networking and developing linkages with other sources of PME support may be required.

PME facilitators helping large organisations need patience and a strong process orientation, as it may take time to enlist participation and build a favourable environment for change. The top leadership will have to buy into everything that is decided to ensure its implementation and it may be necessary to inform all other stakeholders of the decisions taken, requiring appropriate communication channels. If staff capacities are insufficient, training key personnel may be needed, as well as the development of training modules to be delivered after the facilitator has left (see Box 7.8)

ORGANISATIONAL TYPE

The type of organisation (such as NGO, or faith-based organisation) also influences PME practice. While some types overlap, within each differences also exist: a faith-based organisation may thus be 'radical' in its approach, while another may be more welfare oriented. We review faith-based, community-based and network organisations, with their attendant PME facilitation challenges.

FAITH-BASED ORGANISATIONS

Faith-based organisations abound across the world and represent the development arm of institutions, such as a church, or temple, that have a more permanent place in society than many other NGOs. They are often among the oldest structured development organisations within a country's civil society and are well positioned in their linkages with both 'beneficiaries' and government authorities. Stakeholders can have a dual identity, which is not often recognised, such as where a community participant, or a staff member, may also belong to the congregation and can be treated differently in each role. Religious leaders will similarly often emphasise a combination of spiritual and development agenda. This can lead to tension: some will want activities to benefit as many people as possible (just like the cleric offers his message to everybody), but this might compromise effectiveness and run counter to the careful identification of beneficiary groups we see with other development organisations. The consequences for PME need to be studied with

Box 7.9 Notes from the Field: A Mature Faith-based Organisation

Our partner's mission focuses on addressing the spiritual, physical and psycho-social needs of the entire province, in accordance with the Church precept that 'we must serve all mankind'. The key role of our partner, the provincial office, is to fundraise for 'its' parishes and ensure the proper implementation of funded projects. Its large staff complement is attached to various departments and scattered across the area to implement provincial-run projects as well. Most projects and plans are 'rolling'. There is a high level of trust in the team and the staff thrive on their long experiences, but there is little documented organisational memory.

The health programme was recently externally evaluated. This showed that beneficiaries were appreciative and staff busy implementing programmes, but paying little attention to any change in people's lives. The project hardly echoed recent government policy changes in the health sector and little thought was given to possible future directions. This reflected a rudimentary activity-focused M&E system, with limited financial information available for management purposes and a general dearth of documented evidence. The limited availability of financial information in part reflected a long history of warm and easy-going donor relations. Tensions between the Church and the provincial office were also evident, with information restricted to the technical staff and any attempt to access information by others perceived as encroaching on the territory of experts. This behaviour contributed to poor accountability.

Throughout the PME facilitation process, a steady, gradual approach had to be used. It was important to recognise the power of the Church collar and how issues of accountability had to be carefully handled, to avoid any hint of mistrust. Slowly, a management team ethos had to be nurtured, to foster cross-departmental linkages. This enabled the team to start thinking more strategically about future interventions: beyond projects to more cohesive programmes, with a focus on the most vulnerable sections of the population and strengthening community organisations, moving away from a blanket, do-it-all approach and developing M&E procedures accordingly. As facilitators, we also played a go-between role with the donors, encouraging them to coordinate their reporting requirements and to exercise patience with the pace of change.

care, as expectations of the function of PME will differ. The frequent transfers of priests in senior positions, especially in specialised, national-level institutions, may also bring in people with limited experience of working in development-oriented organisations, although professionals are increasingly being hired. The former may have inherited a welfare approach to development, focusing on providing for the needy and marginalised, and a limited emphasis on empowerment. This approach can translate into wide-ranging missions with broadly defined objectives and beneficiary groups (see Box 7.9).

Our experiences with faith-based organisations shows that meaningful discussions can be conducted on the need to show results, sometimes contrary to expectations: religious institutions are performance-oriented; they want to be successful and proud of their achievements, as do other development organisations.

> **Box 7.10 Facilitating PME within a Mature Faith-based Organisation**
>
> ✓ We have found involving the leadership essential when working with such organisations. A discussion of the role of the board (such as a diocesan structure) in PME matters may also be necessary.
>
> ✓ We need to keep in mind the depth of the values informing mission and vision in faith-based organisations: this may limit flexibility in PME processes, although we can often foster a gender-aware approach to PME.
>
> ✓ Where possible, creating cross-departmental linkages is useful, such as by encouraging the inclusion of joint learning and review sessions in the annual plans and of participatory approaches to PME, including community inclusion in periodic review events. We can similarly help reflect on the advantages and disadvantages of multi-sectoral approaches to development work and how a departmental structure can be replicated in PME practice, with appropriate autonomy levels.
>
> ✓ A system for regular contextual analysis and the development of appropriate relationships with other development actors may be important, especially where there is a history of working in isolation.

Although faith-based organisations are sometimes believed to be immutable, they also evolve: the pioneer stage might coalesce around an enterprising priest, or a small group of people united in their faith. Growth is often of a centralising-type (with a critical role for religious leaders) and driven by a desire to reach as many of 'the flock' as possible and, if unchecked, a mature faith-based organisation can become unwieldy, with numerous departments and programmes that do not always see eye-to-eye with religious authorities, or even among themselves. This results in large staff complements, with two overlapping bureaucracies–of the parent religious institution and of its offspring, the development office. The latter is often better endowed than the parent, thanks to long-term funding and technical staff (see Box 7.10).

COMMUNITY-BASED ORGANISATIONS

Community-based organisations occupy an important place in the social and economic landscape of many countries. They are often set up to improve the livelihood of group members and their families and to establish a social support system to help members address their immediate needs (see Box 7.11). A CBO therefore often coalesces around a livelihoods issue and this dictates its form, such as a water users' association, savings and credit group, or village development committee. It may be informal, although the tendency is often towards formalisation, as CBOs increasingly become conduits for donor funds. The availability of skilled and qualified persons to CBOs may be limited, although some, backed by NGOs and other support organisations, may gain in professionalism. A threat may then arise when the supporter begins to control the CBO rather than facilitate it, as when CBO workers are guided by the support organisation and disregard the CBO leadership, especially when the latter's values are not firmly entrenched.

Community-based organisations face their own PME challenges from the beginning, often as small interest groups bound by a strong sense of belonging. Here PME practice is based on trust (reflecting members' enthusiasm, commitment and voluntarism), oral rather

Box 7.11   From Field Notes: A Young CBO

A group met monthly to cultivate (with members contributing labour in turns on individual fields) and prepare local beer for sale. At their second meeting, group members elected a chairperson, a treasurer and a secretary, taking into account their literacy level. The chair was the treasurer's mother, but this was no problem because of the high level of trust within the group. The group held regular meetings and agreed to pay a membership fee of $ 0.5 each. Small exercise books were bought as members' register, minute book and treasurer's record.

Three months later, however, these books were no longer in use, but most members had up-to-date information about the group's history, its achievements, challenges and future plans. The treasurer knew which members had defaulted on their fee. The secretary recalled what had been discussed in the meetings, including some of the statements individuals made. The chairperson knew the history of the group and articulately identified the best and worst months for beer sales.

Facilitating PME processes in such circumstances had to focus on developing short-term, realistic plans, in tune with the group's capacity, rather than lofty vision and mission statements. Pictorial approaches to M&E (to ensure wide membership involvement) were used. As contacts with outsiders grew, however, formal PME practice became more relevant: this first arose when the group became eligible for micro-finance to buy farming tools. From this point on, our facilitation focused on a simple, but structured PME system, with well-kept records.

than written records, and a strong focus on immediate activities and benefits (see Box 7.12). With growth, ownership can be undermined by executive committees that become distant and less accountable to the members, by formalised management systems and PME practice, and by dominating outsiders, including NGO support staff. Enthusiasm will reduce if the benefits of membership become less immediate and sustainability will be under threat when the CBO becomes a vehicle for time-bound project implementation, funded by donors, or governments. These problems may worsen if, as is often the case, capacity-building solely focuses on formalising PME rather than structuring and building on existing practice.

NETWORKS

Networks represent a rapidly growing type of organisation (although not all networking results in an organisation), where PME practice faces unique challenges, since ensuring participation in PME is critical for collective ownership among network members who may have different priorities, interests and value systems (see Box 7.13). Salient issues for PME facilitation with networks include:

1. *Clarity of Language:* This is important from the start of a PME process at three levels: first, the label given to the network (alliance, coalition, consortium, coordinating structure, etc.) has its context-specific meaning and value for the members, expressing expectations and reasons for joining. Verifying this is important, as well as the balance between what members contribute and what they gain from a network. Second, do people refer to the structure, or to the activity? With the former, discussion centres on the organisational form, as a more or less permanent feature. Focusing on the latter implies a perception of networking as a way to learn, collaborate, or exchange information, possibly of a temporary nature. Third, do people refer to the network to include

Box 7.13 Starting Small: Réseau Plaidoyer et Lobby, a Young Lobby Network in Mali

Having attended a series of training events in advocacy work, 15 Malian NGOs decided to establish a lobby platform, with a small secretariat and a one-year pilot programme, mainly to allow members to apply the knowledge gained.

While we were asked, as facilitators, to help Réseau Plaidoyer et Lobby (RPL) set up a modest M&E plan to measure progress and results in its initial year, it was decided to first focus on planning issues. This made sense, as the plan had turned out to be ambitious and expectations ran high. To help members develop a plan better in tune with their capacities, it was agreed to focus on one intervention theme only. The intervention logic was jointly elaborated, carefully reviewing the problem analysis (using a problem tree) and the objectives set. Next, members were stimulated to visualise the changes the network could realistically contribute to and for which it would be responsible. This practical step-by-step approach helped members adjust their expectations to realistic levels, thanks to a good understanding of the complex nature of the chosen theme and of their own limitations. Finally, a first set of indicators was developed, which helped make activities more concrete, going a step further than the earlier vague descriptions.

We avoided discussing the organisational form of the network, in spite of some members' wish to formalise it. It was agreed that, for such a young organisation, efforts in this direction would not be effective as it first needed to develop its own role and capacity, after which formalisation could be given due attention.

the members and the structure, or to the secretariat only? Both these interpretations often coexist in discussions, causing confusion.

2. *Nature of Change, Diversity and Evolution:* Given the frequent lack of precise vision/mission and objectives of networks, PME facilitation often has to start by examining their reason for existence. What was the driving force? What did they want to change? Is the vision similar at the level of the secretariat and the members? How has it changed over the years? Sometimes these changes go unnoticed by the members, as the example from Niger shows (see Box 7.14). Facilitating reflection on members' expectations of the network and its evolving membership is then essential. This may

Box 7.14 History and Reflection as Part of a PME Process with a Regional Network

This partner NGO network was established more than 10 years ago, reflecting the large number of NGOs working in this region of Niger. Its aim was to coordinate their interventions, exchange experiences to increase impact and lobby for NGO-friendly policies. From 13 founding members, the network has quickly grown to its present 50.

The network requested support to better respond to its members' needs and to strengthen its position vis-à-vis other regional actors. A historical analysis tool helped to facilitate reflection on how members had changed in numbers and identity since 1995. This analysis helped the members and executive committee realise that an implicit self-selection had occurred. The network had focused on fundraising and on its professional profile, with its role narrowing to building members' capacities to subcontract government projects. Members had become driven by a wish to become subcontractors, rather than to become a force for social change.

Members had not noticed this evolution. The historical analysis acted as an eye-opener on this changing role and, during a second interaction, it was agreed that the network should both strengthen technical skills as before and act as a catalyst for change, two objectives that are not necessarily mutually exclusive.

have led to a shift in objectives from addressing a single issue (around which many networks form) to multiple ones, often as a result of expanding membership. Membership might itself be diverse. Can the network then cope with these multiple issues? Three dimensions of analysis can guide the facilitator: from inside to outside (what are the relations between the secretariat and the members?), from top to down (who has power and controls resources?) and backwards to forward (what has been the evolution over time?) PME must help to plan and assess these sources of diversity, with indicators to monitor and evaluate them, showing what variety of members and issues is allowed and how the network's in-built heterogeneity can be managed.

3. *Networks, Planning and Learning:* 'Learning' is often a central theme for networks, but practice can tell us a different story. As members are often far apart, and struggling with their own learning and PME practices, what can we reasonably expect of a network? The case of Education et Coordination pour l'Agriculture Durable (ECAD) (see Box 7.15) is instructive in this respect. Where learning processes are emphasised in a network, these need to be planned and monitored, even more so than within member organisations, by looking at what needs to be learnt and how. Second, PME processes must enhance members' participation and ownership. In India, a general evaluation of networks suggested the following sequence: seeking members' inputs well in advance on the issues to be taken up for capacity building, advocacy, or information dissemination; based on this input, develop a list of likely interventions, share it with members, to be returned stating their preferences. The secretariat then collates this data and presents it to the members at a general meeting, where a decision is collectively taken on the intervention, timing and necessary resources. As a result, ownership is formalised and engagement increased. To monitor its performance, the secretariat must still seek regular feedback from the members as to the usefulness and quality of the activities it undertakes. Similarly, members should be asked well in advance to contribute to setting the agenda for network meetings and to scrutinise periodic reports and minutes of executive committee meetings (see Box 7.16).

To conclude, while we have found it essential to start our engagement as PME facilitators by finding out about the nature

Box 7.15 Story Telling and the Challenges of Learning within Networks

Education et Coordination pour l'Agriculture Durable (ECAD), a national NGO network for sustainable agriculture in Cameroon, was founded in 1992. An external evaluation marked the start of a PME facilitation process.

The evaluation not only examined effectiveness, relevance and quality of the programme, but also the division of labour between the secretariat and the membership. This was an issue of concern, as ECAD had struggled to give its members responsibility, rather than push too many tasks onto the plate of a national coordinator heading a modest secretariat. A facilitation step was thus to differentiate between the exclusive tasks of the coordinator and those of the members. The discussion centred on the principle of subsidiarity: what can be done at the 'lower' level should be done there. Later, facilitation focused on the intervention logic of the network programme and the outline of an M&E system. For some components, results at the effect level were elaborated and indicators suggested. ECAD was left to elaborate this for the entire programme.

Two years later, we were involved with ECAD for a third time: little had changed. The network repeated its interventions without much reflection on relevance and effectiveness. No M&E plan existed. The network was not learning; it had become inward looking and stagnant, in part because of its monopoly position in Cameroon. To highlight ECAD's current situation, we invited members to tell their story about important learning experiences. A reflection based on these stories revealed several shortcomings in ECAD's learning process, such as the lack of common learning objectives, of well organised interaction between members, of responsibility for learning and of 'learning about learning'. Story telling proved an important tool to interpret and assess the network's learning process and to demonstrate the dynamic and interactive character of learning in such a structure.

(culture, size, age, ideological background) of the organisation we support, one should not draw hasty conclusions from such classification. A PME assessment process will be necessary to understand PME structure, systems, practices and relevant influencing factors. Such an 'assessment' can best be presented as a 'stocktaking' to convey the message that it is *our* need to learn that

Box 7.16 PME and Networks

✓ We have found trying to verify who owns a network (and in whose interests) an essential starting point in a PME support process. It is also useful to help a network remain aware of in-built tensions and keep discussing them, bringing them in the open for resolution.

✓ It is helpful to make networks alert to the challenges associated with a great diversity of members, or themes, making it difficult to satisfy all members' expectations. More focus to start with may be appropriate.

✓ Debates on organisational form should be avoided in the initial stage of development, by highlighting the advantages of a focus on activities first. The strengths and drawbacks of a formal structure can be usefully discussed at a later stage.

✓ We can also help networks realise that member coordination and relations are essential and should not be considered a costly overhead. Networks often must realise that their members are their target group, or clients.

✓ Who 'does' the PME? The secretariat might be the logical choice, but there might be other options: the general assembly, the founders, groups of members, etc.

is being met at this point and thus avoid any danger of intimidating those involved.

8

PME SUPPORT AND PROGRAMME DIVERSITY

Development organisations have, over the years, expanded their action into large-scale service delivery, relief work, advocacy and policy influencing. Their work also increasingly involves building the capacity of other organisations, including NGOs, local governments and community groups. This chapter, to complement earlier case studies and to follow our customising approach, explores some of the particular PME challenges associated with such interventions, especially with advocacy, capacity-building, conflict and peace, and emergency programmes.

SECTOR OF INTERVENTION

The sector in which an organisation intervenes will influence its PME practice. Thus, organisations working on health issues often use universally accepted indicators and elaborate systems, such as for

Box 8.1 Sectors of Intervention

Sectors in which 'Best Practices' are Well Known and Accepted
Organisations here implement activities according to proven product or service specifications. They focus on outputs as their most important results, knowing that these outputs will almost certainly lead to the expected results at higher level. In the health sector, for instance, a vaccination programme follows a prescribed protocol to achieve the best quality outputs and leads to reduced rates of morbidity, or mortality, caused by a specific disease. Similar examples exist in the micro-finance sector, where standard internal procedures are followed to guarantee good repayment rates. In these cases, output information may be sufficient for internal learning and external information.

This will need to be occasionally supplemented by M&E at higher levels if new approaches or services need testing, as effects and impacts have become uncertain. Thus, a health institution may run a child nutrition programme, with its protocols in terms choice of food items, energy intake in relation to age and sex, etc. Experience might, however, be insufficient with regard to behaviour or attitude: what exactly drives mothers to select and prepare food differently? This makes effect M&E essential.

Sectors with a More Experimental Character
Information on outputs will not be sufficient here, because achieving them, even if they are of high quality and efficiency, is no guarantee to having effects and impact. As there are no best practices, organisations do not have a guide as to the correct choice of outputs. This is true for, say, many farmer-training programmes, where market conditions are often insufficiently considered and access to basic inputs is lacking. Capacity-building efforts to enhance leadership skills through training provide another example, as they often fail to achieve results when various factors are not taken into account at the design stage (or the mix of activities is incorrect). In these cases, output monitoring is insufficient: M&E at effect and impact levels is essential for learning, as the best practices still need to be identified.

assessing morbidity rates or the knowledge, attitudes and practices of a beneficiary group. Organisations working in the micro-credit field similarly often adopt sophisticated monitoring systems, partly because of the relative ease of monitoring quantitative aspects of this

Box 8.2 PME and the Pitfalls of Multi-sectoral Organisations

Many NGOs and faith-based development organisations have, over the years, embraced a multi-sectoral approach, sometimes also referred to as 'holistic' or 'integrated'. This has often been a response to working in isolation in marginalised areas without social and economic services, or to respond to the prescriptions of donors, that view the marginalisation of the poor as the result of several interlocking factors.

The challenges to PME here include the lack of good references or benchmarks to measure the performance of multi-sectoral programmes, as compared to specialised organisations, which can benefit from best practices developed for a specific sector. While some multi-sectoral organisations are effective (especially those with experienced, specialised departments), others face the challenges of overambition (reflecting a lack of technical insights). Seeing themselves as unique actors (especially faith-based organisations that stress their permanence), with an emphasis on direct implementation, makes collaboration with other organisations difficult. The reality, however, is often that other organisations have emerged and decentralisation has taken root, making collaboration imperative. The lack of clear focus and an island mentality can hinder PME facilitation. Pointing this out, by discussing the advantages and drawbacks of specialisation versus integration, can provide a useful first step.

work, such as saving volume or recovery rates, and partly because there is an urgency to monitor results in a field that is fraught with financial uncertainties (see Box 8.1).

Conversely, organisations working in more experimental areas, or towards more qualitative change processes, such as changing power structures, or raising awareness on rights, will find it more difficult to institutionalise PME practice. Difficulties might arise from challenges in defining clear results and indicators to measure such processes. When PME facilitators struggle to clarify these issues, it strengthens a perception that PME tools are unsuitable for these sectors and one then hears that 'PME systems focus on targets, ignoring processes'. This may be partly true, as a consequence of inadequate PME systems, and is an important area for us to find answers to.

When development organisations work in several sectors simultaneously, this presents its own PME challenges (see Box 8.2), but we now turn to specific sector interventions, chosen to share particular PME challenges. These are sectors that often display an experimental character, requiring organisations to place learning high on their agenda, in spite of the difficulty to estimate results because of unpredictability and weak cause-effect relationships.

ADVOCACY WORK

Particular PME challenges arise when working with an organisation engaged in advocacy or policy-influencing. These include:

PROBLEM ANALYSIS AND PLANNING

Planning advocacy work is challenging, including having to select the set of activities needed to achieve results and to predict the time required to achieve them. Advocacy involves influencing a power structure, persons, or institutions, that are largely beyond the control of the implementing organisation, and making specific plans with rigidly defined results can be unrealistic. Such projects usually require, besides alternate scenarios which are rarely developed, a dynamic planning framework with frequent monitoring and a facility to modify timelines and plan additional activities while keeping the result in focus.

Box 8.3 Defining Results: Suggestive or More Tangible?

✓ An Indian NGO held a dialogue with community organisation leaders, asking them to think of the type of rights-based action they may take up in their respective areas. Thereafter the NGO articulated a result statement in the planning document as: 'At least 20 out of 25 organisations each year address at least four issues (such as user rights over village ponds or obtaining public distribution cards for families below the poverty line)'.

✓ AF India implemented a watershed management programme, with a number of accomplishments in terms of advocacy and policy changes, including: adoption of a people-centred participatory approach in planning and implementing a government watershed development programme; considering the village as the unit for watershed (rather than the 500 ha of land previously used by the government); and allowing community organisations autonomy in planning and sanctioning plans below a specified financial ceiling.

✓ During a planning event, an Indian organisation engaging parliamentarians on child-focused laws and their implementation was reluctant to put down tangible results, let alone quantitative targets, because of the lack of control over the policy-makers. The facilitator, however, insisted that this was both possible and necessary to challenge those involved and to assess progress in relation to set targets. As the discussion progressed, a practical solution was worked out: the organisation would adopt a step-by-step approach, setting challenging targets as it went along, detailing time, staffing and budgetary requirements. A target would thus read: at least 40 people's representatives motivated to raise a question in Parliament. On achieving this, in full or in part, the organisation would set a target for the next higher result. In this manner the organisation would work step-by-step, and with targets to motivate itself.

It is thus possible to define clear and tangible advocacy results, describing desirable changes, as part of a long-term policy change. Close monitoring in an advocacy programme, from a results perspective, beyond completion of activities, is vitally important. This demands a thorough problem analysis of, say, all relevant policy issues, including how they may impede sustained results for the target group.

Planning advocacy work is also difficult if it is to be carried out by one organisation, but with results articulated on its behalf by another. A lead NGO might thus prepare a project proposal on behalf of a network, or a CBO that is meant to implement the advocacy agenda. The NGO then faces the dilemma of preparing specific result statements, without the participation of other stakeholders. Even if community representatives join the dialogue, they may not be able to predict which actions their organisation will take up. In such a situation, suggested outcomes, rather than exhaustive results might be appropriate, although these cannot substitute for a comprehensive problem analysis (see Box 8.3).

FOCUS ON ACTIVITIES AND M&E OF QUALITATIVE CHANGE

Unsurprisingly, therefore, many organisations remain at the activity level when planning advocacy work: a rally to advocate for child rights, for instance, which, when completed, is reported

Box 8.4 Organisations Involved in Advocacy Work

✓ Attention needs to be given at the outset to a thorough problem analysis. This may include joint analysis with beneficiary groups and other stakeholders to identify expected changes. Such joint reflection should lead to concrete examples of changes, for which the implementing organisation can take responsibility.

✓ As facilitators, we must emphasise the need to define clear and realistic results and plan interventions that match the organisation's capacity. Specific and localised lobby issues allow for easier tracking of results, with fewer attribution problems.

✓ Advocacy work requires constant adjustments of plans, objectives and interventions: it is important to explain this, even where a clear result statement has been developed at the onset of a programme.

✓ A keen, objective eye is often needed to estimate the level of change achieved and follow-up action required. It may be worthwhile to involve third party monitors from within or outside the organisation to assess this.

✓ Where an advocacy project involves more than one organisation, involving the different partners in defining results and strategies, and in monitoring results, is desirable. Networks analysis tools can help in this respect.

as a 'success', irrespective of whether this leads to any real change. The emotional satisfaction of having organised an event attended by thousands of people, or prominent politicians, is of little consequence if the promise made to effect a policy change is not kept. In either case, a follow-up action plan is needed to ensure that the expected change does happen. The challenge of monitoring an advocacy project, however, stems largely from the qualitative nature of most results, such as opinion building among different stakeholders (see Box 8.4).

EMERGENCY PROGRAMMES

While emergencies vary in their causes, speed and consequences, they highlight specific PME challenges, also reflected in facilitation work:

THE NEED FOR A SWIFT RESPONSE

Emergencies, such as an earthquake, or a severe famine, call for a speedy response to save lives, treat injuries and trauma, to bring the community to a tolerable situation as quickly as possible and may be to help it prepare for the next emergency. The time available for elaborate planning is limited and this can also lead implementing organisations to resist drawing up full-fledged funding proposals. An unclear proposal, however, remains problematic for a donor, especially where reporting norms to a 'back donor' remain stringent.

ENSURING RELEVANCE, QUALITY AND ACCOUNTABILITY

While aid may be available, the agencies that get involved, unless they have a specific capacity for emergency response, are often local organisations with little experience of such situations. Some excellent relief work was carried out after the recent tsunami, for instance, but there were also lapses in *relevance* (affected persons, for instance, refused food without fish at the cost of being underfed), *quality* (there were reports of poor planning of temporary settlements leading to water logging and fires) and *accountability* (some organisations failed to maintain proper accounts, list of beneficiaries, or supporting documents) (see Box 8.5).

Box 8.5 PME Facilitation and the Tsunami Emergency in South Asia: Three Challenges

Facilitating PME processes for 15 NGOs in a relief phase and 15 in a rehabilitation phase proved an enriching experience from three perspectives:

✓ The context: Urgency and an ever-changing context demanded quick and flexible plans, but these also had to be coherent and effective for sustainable results. Planning was challenged by a multitude of agencies willing to provide services: these had to give details of the funds being received, their purpose and the location of use through the media. NGOs undertook not to duplicate services amongst themselves and a network was quickly and successfully forged to coordinate with governments.

✓ Ideological and methodological diversity: The crisis brought together relief agencies clear about their service delivery role. Others had a longer term perspective and responded with long-term plans. Still others saw the problem from a rights-based perspective and developed plans to challenge governments on the distribution of relief, resisted the displacement of families and challenged international NGOs on practices they perceived as inappropriate. The PME facilitators had to maintain neutrality, accepting the need for ideological diversity, retaining flexibility to facilitate the different agencies and encouraging synergy among them where possible.

✓ Capacities and attitudes of implementing agencies: The local NGOs could manage projects, but had limited experience of disaster response and handling large funds. While the commitment of donor funds helped to plan well in some cases, in others, agencies planned in a hurry (often to meet urgent needs, but at times as a pretext to get money quickly). Occasional donor pressure added to the sense of urgency. This compromised the quality of plans and the PME facilitators had to convince the NGOs to adopt a longer term 'success' point of view, using much 'hand holding' in doing so.

Focus on Activities, Monitoring and Reporting

A focus on activities rather than results is most striking in emergency situations where plans and reports highlight, say, the 'number of people provided with food, shelter, water and sanitation', rather than whether there was 'success in preventing disease and death'. When large-scale emergencies draw much public and media attention, specific programme and financial reports need to be prepared to account and demonstrate results. Implementing agencies struggling with harsh, dynamic, even surreal conditions may, however, see monitoring, documentation and reporting as an unnecessary bother.

Thinking beyond the Emergency

Providing free handouts to affected persons and prolonging relief work can reflect an inability to assess when to get the community moving on its own. When relief winds down, unless it is in a complex emergency, such as drought coupled with civil war, planning must gradually shift from quick action to well thought-out and strategic rehabilitation interventions (see Box 8.6). Field realities at times dictate that this be done quickly: after the recent tsunami in South Asia, for instance, a gap developed between the end of the relief phase and the start of the rehabilitation efforts. People became restless, expecting quick economic rehabilitation and permanent houses. It is also often after an emergency that communities and governments start thinking about emergency preparedness. If the planning process is not well facilitated, preparedness will remain a missing element in plans that only focus on immediate relief and rehabilitation efforts, neglecting preparations against future threats (see Box 8.7).

Box 8.6 A Flexible Response to Emergency: The Drought Cycle Management Model in East Africa

While droughts recur in many arid and semi-arid areas around the world, local land users have developed ways to cope and minimise risks. With the neglect of such communities and their land use systems, however, coping strategies break down and people get trapped in a cycle of increased poverty and vulnerability. Since the recent droughts in East Africa, many organisations have gained experience in dealing with such disasters and have developed a 'drought cycle management model'.

Droughts, contrary to some other disasters, are slow in announcing themselves. Effective M&E (including early warning systems [EWS] must therefore help to raise the alarm. The underlying premise of the model is that droughts are normal phenomena: they come and go, some develop into full-fledged disasters, others do not. They also undergo stages, with specific activities (such as in animal health, natural resource management and conflict resolution) fitting in a relief-rehabilitation-development continuum. The monitoring system warns of imminent stress and is linked to drought preparedness and response. Organisations must be prepared to adapt their intervention to these stages and to collaborate with others, where required. They increasingly understand the need to integrate these stages of the model, which is now widely accepted in the region. In Kenya, the government has accepted the model as the basic response model for droughts and its use has become an indicator of quality organisations.

For the PME facilitator, particular issues arise, including the degree of familiarity of a partner organisation with the model; and how traditional EWS knowledge and local coping strategies can be analysed and recognised as a relevant component in a total drought monitoring system. But there are other issues too, such as the continuation of M&E during the emergency stage, given the pressure on staff and time at this stage, to reflect on the efficiency and effectiveness of emergency operations and improve on the quality of contingency plans. Other questions to consider include: who might be willing to pay for such M&E system, especially when there is no drought, and how can PME capacity-building best take into account the emergency stage of the drought cycle, which may offer good opportunities to measure the impact of emergency operations?

Box 8.7 Organisations Involved in Emergency Situations

✓ Continuing PME during emergencies is necessary. Emergency situations demand guidelines for implementation, adherence to certain operating principles related to timeliness, quality assurance, maintaining focus on the vulnerable and marginalised, stakeholder participation, cultural sensitivity, etc. Guidelines on basic record keeping and monitoring to avoid subsequent problems with accountability and reporting are also required. Donors and facilitators with past emergency experience can play a useful role in this respect. Staff daily diaries may help, as they leave a record even after the authors have left.

✓ PME facilitators need to highlight the need for clear plans to ensure effective implementation, monitoring and reporting. They can point out that the purpose of any intervention is its result and not the activity alone and should facilitate this articulation in all plans and reports.

✓ To allow those concerned with field-level action to work uninterrupted, it may be desirable to have separate staff for monitoring and reporting, provided the conditions have been created to ensure acceptance of their feedback. They can also undertake other tasks, such as networking with government and other organisations.

✓ When planning the transition from relief to rehabilitation, facilitators may have to contend with contradictory pressures, such as from implementing NGOs wanting speedy action and from donors seeking assurances about strategy and plans. Facilitators can supplement the perspective of implementing agencies to help judge when to call off free handouts. Even if fully fledged rehabilitation interventions are not envisaged, there may be scope of food-for-work, or cash-for-work initiatives.

✓ While it is important to integrate emergency preparedness in many development initiatives, it is of little use to make provisions for actions without the requisite capacity, which is often lacking because of limited previous experience in this field. This calls for capacity-building to mainstream emergency preparedness in plans, for which experienced facilitators, who are familiar with this sector, are best placed.

CONFLICTS AND PEACE-BUILDING

While conflicts surround us almost permanently, some of the unique challenges arising from facilitating PME in their more extreme manifestations include:

DIFFICULTY IN GAUGING RESULTS

Results are uncertain in the best of circumstances, but lack of control on outcomes in conflict situations is greater. A partner organisation may find understanding a community and its internal dynamics especially challenging, if this community and its leaders are also party to the conflict. Where a conflict is wider, the organisation

Box 8.8 Conflict and the Need for Flexible PME in Colombia

Colombia has for long been ravaged by civil war with 'leftist' and 'rightist' groups violently battling each other, often at the expense of the civilian population. While it is almost impossible to have a neutral position, NGOs in collaboration with churches, companies and grass-roots organisations try to engage with the warring groups to end conflict. Any debate is valued as it carries the potential to reduce tensions, although the context in which these debates take place, including the relations between the different parties, changes rapidly.

Programme planning is difficult in such circumstances: plans have to be changed rapidly. Successes have been achieved, but how can they be evaluated when plans constantly change? Monitoring and evaluation then tends to focus more on hypotheses, or assumptions, behind activities or plans instead of on activities only. Was the assumption correct, why, why not? Was it possible to implement the plan? Were we correct to collaborate with particular groups? Who was supportive? Who was present at the debates? Who was not? What did they say? How quickly could we move?

In this situation, flexibility of PME must be emphasised with a focus on constant context monitoring, being prepared for the sudden and unexpected, and on short-term planning frameworks.

may not have the reach to act on its resolution, but may have to focus on protecting people from its harmful effects, or ensuring as normal a life in the community as possible. Estimating results is even more difficult when, as is often the case, the conflict is fast evolving. Change is rarely a linear progression in normal circumstances, and is almost never so in conflict situations (see Box 8.8).

MULTI-STAKEHOLDER SITUATION

Unlike a service delivery programme in a relatively peaceful situation, several stakeholders in a conflict situation might be left out, or not influenced, by the project of the intervening organisation. This complicates all-inclusive planning; let alone consulting them if they are inaccessible or have divergent convictions.

DIFFICULT CIRCUMSTANCES

As PME facilitators, we must appreciate that our partners are operating in difficult circumstances, where they may be affected by the conflict themselves and their personal safety is threatened. The desire to engage in elaborate planning may thus be minimal, despite the fact that it may be all the more crucial to effectively address a complicated situation (see Box 8.9).

PME OF CAPACITY-BUILDING

While capacity-building for PME is at the core of this book, as facilitators, we may find ourselves supporting other capacity-building programmes and organisations. Their numbers have grown with the increasing recognition that capacity, or 'social capital', must be built to sustain results over time. Work in this area brings the following PME-related issues to the fore:

WHAT CHANGE IS SOUGHT?

A capacity-building effort is ultimately meant to change the lives of the 'beneficiaries'. This can involve a long chain of events: thus,

Box 8.9   Organisations Involved in Peace-building and Conflict Resolution Work

✓ Specific and realistic results beyond activities can often be planned, a dynamic review and adjustment process put in place, and several optional plans reflecting possible changes in the conflict situation developed. While flexibility of PME and short-term planning frameworks are often called for, facilitators can help clarify the long-term results, for example, conflict resolution, or protection of the community in a conflict zone. Strategies and short-term results will be defined accordingly.

✓ It is often best to avoid monitoring and reporting systems with a sole emphasis on linear and numerical change, and allow space to explain the changing context and the adverse impact it may have on an otherwise high-quality intervention. Constant context monitoring and preparedness for the unexpected is essential. This requires innovative facilitators who can use a process approach to reflect the circumstances.

✓ Rather than measuring outcomes, especially if the work is directly related to resolving a crisis or reducing tension it may be important to monitor and analyse the process, the quality of efforts and short-term outputs. Particular attention should be given to the appropriateness of the methods of data collection: interviews about success and results may, for instance, make stakeholders uncomfortable, but they may be willing to reflect on the status of the community before and after an intervention. Facilitators need to create the right kind of ambience for this, including the mental framework and a clear understanding of the planning framework.

✓ Similarly, facilitators need to be empathetic in their approach: the desire to construct an elaborate monitoring system may be absent among implementing agency workers in a complex situation, although this should not be construed as lack of willingness to monitor. Some organisations working in conflict situations may have a strong tradition of collective reflection and analysis of their work. This must be recognised, encouraged, or initiated, if not already present.

for people to benefit, a development programme must be relevant and of good quality. For this to happen, programme planners must be able to plan effectively and the implementers must have

Box 8.10 Capacity-building: Dealing with the Challenge of Tracing Impact

Organisation development (OD) practitioners, mainly from the African continent, recently met to review their experiences in monitoring and evaluating their work. Much discussion centred on the desirability and feasibility of monitoring and evaluating the impact of organisational support at the ultimate beneficiary level. While this was recognised as challenging (because of cost, attribution problems and because the degree of legitimacy of the OD provider at this level is questionable), it was agreed that it was desirable to show, however imprecisely, that support does produce a change where it ultimately matters and to be accountable to partner organisations and their beneficiaries.

This could be done by focusing on traces of support work at the beneficiary level; on a contribution to change, or on a change that a partner organisation might wish to see as a result of the support intervention. This required 'treading carefully, not being too ambitious and retaining a level of humility, looking for indications of impact and avoiding any information overload'. The key was felt to reside in respecting ownership and supporting partners trace changes and document them themselves, by building their

(Box 8.10 Contd.)

(Box 8.10 Contd.)

M&E capacity, co-designing M&E with them and even with their beneficiary groups. It could be done by triangulating methods, both formal and informal, that demand little time/money:

✓ A small sample, developing one or two case studies.
✓ Dialogues, joint analysis, helping clients/beneficiaries collect information.
✓ Meetings (accompanied by the partner organisation) with one of their beneficiary group at the outset and after an intervention.
✓ Stories of change, annual reports of partner organisations, joint visits and occasional visits/telephone calls with previous partners.

Box 8.11 Capacity-building: The Need for Participation and Contextual Analysis

ICCO and CORDAID, two Dutch funding agencies, have supported a capacity-building programme in 10 countries in Eastern Europe and Central Asia, to help local support organisations develop their capacity to assist other partner organisations in a sustainable manner. This idea, while good in principle, was compromised by insufficient analysis of contextual differences, in part because this was a new region of work for ICCO and CORDAID.

Organisational development support suffered from this. Thus, gender training given to women from the 10 countries together, while meant to allow participants to benefit from South–South exchanges, failed to recognise that they were far apart in terms of information, awareness and aspirations.

A programme evaluation recommended the involvement of the local organisations in needs assessment and planning, which had, in this case, been carried out by the donor agencies alone. The programme would then better meet needs, as locally perceived. It was also concluded that the programme objectives were vague, which made M&E difficult. Although capacity-building is less 'concrete' than many other interventions, efforts should go into defining measurable objectives and targets in order to identify results.

the knowledge, skills and motivation to implement effectively. Some capacity-building processes contribute very indirectly to programme effectiveness, such as with a strategic planning process, training event, or policy formulation workshop. Monitoring the quality of a capacity-building intervention calls for keen observation and receiving objective feedback from the users of the support given. Better knowledge, or skills levels, can be assessed by documenting and comparing 'before' and 'after' situations. Monitoring may also need to involve other stakeholders, such as local governments, funders and local communities. A donor agency representative can, for instance, provide useful feedback on the quality of proposals and reports. Improvements within the partner organisation, including capacity to manage and change, as a result of a capacity-building process, can more easily be measured than at the final beneficiary level. Where possible, however, M&E at the partner level should document any change in its values and impact-making processes (see Boxes 8.10 and 8.11).

IT ALL TAKES TIME...

There are different levels of achievement in capacity-building: a first level of results often deals with clarity of concepts, or enhanced knowledge. It is often unrealistic for capacity-building planners to assume that a short-term intervention, such as a training workshop aimed at familiarisation with particular techniques, will lead to their adoption by trainees. For skills to be developed, sufficient practice needs to be provided and supported with adequate feedback. Initially, practice might need much guidance and lead to better conceptual understanding, rather than better skills and confidence in being able to perform the task independently. Planning capacity-building interventions of sufficient length, intensity and approach is thus important: a capacity-building agenda will often have to include a process where participants meet the facilitators for assessments and follow-ups, giving ample opportunities to practice and improve (see Box 8.12).

Box 8.12 Organisations Involved in Capacity-building Work

✓ Facilitators need to point out that the success of a capacity-building initiative depends on strategies that go beyond any training room and is best measured by estimating change at the final beneficiary level.

✓ Monitoring capacity-building work calls for assessment at different levels, different times and using different tools. Monitoring can, for instance, include: suitability and quality of the intervention, results achieved in terms of concepts clarified and skills improved and their application.

✓ At the partner organisation level, one can agree on what will be monitored: the facilitator can then help the partner develop its own M&E system. Several tools and approaches can be used, including various organisational assessment tools, quick scans, joint reflections and context reviews.

✓ Organisations often describe the result of capacity-building in terms of people becoming more active, participatory, enthusiastic, or having gained knowledge and awareness: this is difficult and vague to measure. However, at the planning stage, what can one imagine seeing the people, whose capacity has been built, do? How would they practically show this new state? Such questions can help planners identify specific and realistic results, which can be qualified and/or quantified.

✓ Skills to assess qualitative change objectively will be very helpful. Any cynicism in failing to recognise results such as increased knowledge, understanding or confidence, use of knowledge and change in the quality and quantity of work is evidently to be avoided.

9

THE FACILITATOR'S APPROACH

Having shared our experiences, we can now conclude by reflecting on the overall facilitation process. We recall our wish to avoid a blueprint approach to PME, so that organisational and contextual specificities are fully taken into account. We also wish to move PME away from a single focus on upward accountability, to a learning approach. We have therefore proposed a process approach that is tailor-made, flexible, inward as well as outward-looking. How can a PME process be developed to reflect these intentions in practice.

A POSSIBLE PROCESS

We keep in mind that the function and location of any PME system in any particular organisation will determine its contents and the processes used. However, some basic steps or stages *can* be envisaged, highlighting the importance of *preparation*:

ESTABLISHING THE ORIGIN OF THE REQUEST AND THE NATURE OF THE NEED

This first step is likely to entail consultations with different stakeholders within and 'around' the partner organisation. It may be part of an original orientation visit, a brief PME overview, and could include a field visit. If needs felt by the partner do not cover all those that we, as facilitators, have identified, some negotiations will be required: can the partner accept our preliminary analysis, can they afford to have possible additional needs addressed? Key issues to keep in mind:

1. Does the request for support originate from the partner, its beneficiaries, donors, or the facilitators?

2. The answer may inform the next steps in the process: if a PME system is (or is perceived as) a donor imposition, for instance, attitudes will differ from a situation where a partner identifies its own needs and contacts a facilitator for help directly. Low expectations and an element of unquestioning gratitude might also creep in, if facilitation comes free.

3. Are felt needs masking any others that may not be so apparent to our prospective partner?

SHARING OUR CREDENTIALS AND APPROACH TO PME AND ASSESSING OURSELVES

As part of the introductory visit, we can 'market' ourselves, outlining the interests, principles and values informing our support process. At this point, we should suggest our areas of strengths and identify areas where we do not have expertise. We should also market our approach to PME: why it may take some time to address needs, why a contextual approach is important, etc. Based on this presentation, a partner can decide if, when and generally how it would like to improve its PME processes. Key questions to remember include:

1. Can we competently handle all the partner's expectations? Have we clarified that, while 'holistic', what we propose is to strengthen PME, not an all-encompassing organisation development process?

2. Does the partner understand and trust us? What opportunities can we suggest for knowing us better?

SUGGESTING A POSSIBLE PME STRENGTHENING PROCESS

This may take place during a subsequent visit to the partner, when different options, time frames and their financial implications will be discussed. The rationale for each step in the proposed process must be clearly understood. Some reflection issues are:

1. If the PME overview has been conclusive, what could be the next steps in the process?

2. Could this tag onto other existing processes, such as an evaluation, or strategic planning exercise? What are the implications of these processes for approaches and next steps?

3. How can these steps be shared so that ownership of the strengthening process is as wide as possible?

ORGANISATIONAL AND PME ASSESSMENTS

These will include culture, history, activities, structure and systems. These assessments—organisational and PME—are essential to further develop the proposed strengthening plan and to prepare a *PME intervention baseline.* Key questions include:

1. How well do we understand the context informing the PME strengthening work? Is PME, for instance, seen as an opportunity for learning?

2. How clear are we on the strengths and weaknesses of the partner's current PME practice and that of its own partners? How can we build on any existing practice, however informal, and use it as entry point?

Canvassing for Support, Finalising and Agreeing on the Support Process

Our understanding is growing, proposals are firming up: we can now elicit support. First, by convincing the leaders in the organisation to commit time and resources to the proposed PME strengthening. A suggested final plan can then be agreed upon. This could be codified into an agreement, or terms of reference, outlining the roles and responsibilities of both facilitator and partner organisation(s), as well as expected milestones, processes, timelines and budgets. This may also require a donor agreement, should external resources be needed. Key issues at this stage are:

1. Considering the assessments mentioned here and the feedback on our earlier proposals, what have we learnt from the partner and the other stakeholders we consulted?

2. What adjustments have to be made?

Implementing the Plan (Part 1)

This only now brings us to the conclusion of the preparatory phase. The first implementation steps may include events to:

1. Clarify terminology.
2. Discuss and agree on organisational pre-conditions for successful PME implementation.
3. Appreciate the external contextual factors that influence PME.

Implementing the Plan (Part 2)

This could include a variety of training, coaching and mentoring events, involving different participants at different times. Here are examples:

1. Participatory development of a PME framework.
2. An output-oriented training event to identify community-based indicators, or an operational plan.

Two PME facilitators, including a donor representative, undertook process-driven PME capacity-building with six Indian partner organisations. This was a learning experience for the facilitators as much as for the partners.

The first step was for the donor representative to explore PME capacity-building and enquire if partners saw a need and interest in this. With an affirmative answer (even though the facilitators were aware that this may be under donor pressure), all six organisations, their leaders and their staff were met together. This was to assess capacity-building needs as much as establishing credentials and breaking the ice. There were four categories of responses: instant rapport with two partners; a warming up by the end of the visit for two others; one sceptical ('We would be happy if you could turn things around, but hope that you outsiders will understand our context and culture'); and one welcoming the facilitators, but feeling that there would be little to learn. In a concluding meeting with all partners, a customised agenda for each was nevertheless agreed upon.

The process took off and produced good results, with partners open to the support. One clear indicator was further requests, even without the support of the same donor. Others were the use of learning points and

(Box 9.1 Contd.)

(Box 9.1 Contd.)

enquiries about subsequent visits. This acceptance was due, according to external evaluators, to 'the methodology adopted by the facilitators that had emphasized respect, rapport and a complete recognition of the social credibility and relevance of every trainee organisation involved'. Partners also vouched for this in their feedback about the facilitators' accessibility to meet their needs.

The assimilation of learning occurred because of synergy between the meticulous attention paid by the facilitators to the training methodology and the tailor-made content: 'The methodology emphasised conceptual clarity and allowed space for simulations during the training period. The engagements between the trainee organisation and the facilitators seem to go far beyond training, or even capacity-building. Rather, they have really been a cause for organisation building/rebuilding'.

3. Review of financial systems.

4. Joint development of M&E tools for data collection, including practice sessions.

5. Help with data analysis and decision-making.

6. Facilitate re-planning.

7. Support for building the required organisational infrastructure.

8. Refinement and review of the partner's programme.

Monitoring and Evaluating the Process

As the main task gets accomplished, this is the time for M&E by us and our partners, to ask some key questions, such as:

1. Can we keep several fingers on the PME pulse? What does looking at the PME intervention baseline (the fourth step–Organisational and PME Assessment) tell us? (See also the section on capacity-building, Chapter 8.) What has been learnt from the whole exercise? Was it cost-effective?

2. Do we stop at this point, if little progress has been made, or do we need to look for help as our capacity is stretched?

POST-INTERVENTION REVIEWS AND SUPPORT

This is possibly the most important step: ensuring that PME has life breathed into it and that PME systems are sustainable, while local ownership is complete. However:

1. What adjustments have to be made?
2. What new challenges are emerging and what further support might be needed?
3. Is consensus for re-building required?

FACILITATORS' APPROACHES AND ATTITUDES

This section briefly outlines how we can help partners move through the process suggested here. The reader is referred to the 'tips' provided throughout the previous chapters for further details.

COMMUNICATION AND FACILITATION

Given the cultural dimension of PME, communicating in a sensitive manner, across organisational cultures as well as national ones, assumes much importance. As facilitators, we need not only to be good cross-cultural communicators, to understand the multicultural contexts in which a partner organisation operates, but also to use any power we yield as facilitator humbly and wisely.

We have found sharing comparative experiences useful in this respect. This provides opportunities to stress a value-driven process, such as incorporating gender equity aspects. This is subject to the partner's consent, but we can mirror in our own attitude the much desired open learning approach we seek to promote in our partners. At times too, a critical, even provocative stance can be effective and justified, if mutual trust allows. This includes being sceptical (as to reported results, for instance), as well as stressing innovation and risk-taking.

A Flexible Process with Carefully Chosen Tools and Methodologies

We need to facilitate a process that is not reduced to a series of predetermined steps in a fixed order. The process needs to follow partner-specific needs—reflecting the type of organisation, age, requirements, skill levels, etc. It also needs to allow for constant adaptation and improvisation.

An important challenge here concerns the choice of methodologies and tools, making judicious choices, according to specific circumstances. Similarly, we need to remember that developing PME processes cannot solely rely on training workshops; indeed mentoring and coaching will often be critical to ensure that such processes are sustained.

An Inclusive, Participatory Process

For a PME system to be owned and sustained, the widest possible involvement in its design and use is required. We therefore need to promote both our 'total organisational' and learning approch to PME, and to create and exploit all opportunities for participation of women and men in as many stages of the process as possible. As facilitators, this may include adopting a 'doing and showing' stance, and helping managers develop an attitude that helps all levels of staff—including the 'juniors'—and partner communities realise that they have the competence to participate in PME processes.

Local Management

A PME support process can benefit from the support of a representative 'change committee' (or person) from within the organisation to guide, monitor and assess it and act as our counterpart. This committee can then document what changes can be noted, what are new obstacles, suggest next steps and play a role in sustaining any agreed PME initiative. Such a committee, however, has to be well anchored in the organisation and feedback mechanisms are all-important. This is a valuable accountability mechanism for the PME facilitator vis-à-vis the partner.

INSERTION INTO ONGOING PLANS

Integrating M&E as part of regular work plans is a necessary condition to develop it as an effective and accepted tool for all concerned. This can require a considerable investment in time and possibly money, and a revision of daily activity schedules. As facilitators, we need to keep this constantly in mind: how can the process become a normal part of our partner organisation's daily practice?

SEEKING SIMPLICITY

Clear, simple, non-expert: do we need to say more?

We close by restating the importance of the values that underpin any PME strengthening process: if PME is essential for organisational survival, our efforts can only be justified when vibrant civil organisations continue to commit themselves to improving the lives of the poor and marginalised. PME must play a central role in ensuring that such a commitment is upheld, both by our partner organisations and by us, the facilitators.

FURTHER READING

Here are a few sources which we have found useful, with a brief description of contents, arranged according to the chapters of this book.

Chapter 2

- OECD (2003). 'Glossary of Key Terms in Evaluations and Results-based Management'. Developed by the DAC Working Party on Aid Evaluation. This work represents an attempt to arrive at a common vocabulary. This glossary includes French and Spanish terms. Available at www.oecd.org/dac.

- Rubin, F. (1995). *A Basic Guide to Evaluation for Development Workers*. Oxford: Oxfam. This short text clarifies basic terms and processes, with a focus on how to plan an evaluation and the uses of different types of evaluations.

- Roche, C. (1999). *Impact Assessment for Developing Agencies: Learning to Value Change*. Oxford: Oxfam. This book shows how impact assessment can be integrated in all programme stages. It starts with a theoretical overview, covers the design of impact assessment processes and the choice of tools and methods. A variety of case studies highlight a range of approaches to impact assessment.

Chapter 3

- IC Consult. 'Short' and 'elaborate' organisational assessment scans are available from IC Consult and associated documents (such as instructions to users) can be downloaded from www.icconsult.nl. These are useful to illustrate the 'total organisational approach' to PME and to stimulate joint reflection with management and staff. The frameworks can be used for any type of organisation, but need to be contextualised. They are also relevant when planning and monitoring/evaluating capacity-building initiatives as they can be used periodically.

- Earl, S., F. Carden and T. Smutylo (2001). *Outcome Mapping: Building Learning and Reflection into Development Programs.* Ottawa: IDRC. Also available at www.idrc.ca. This book 'shifts away from assessing the products of a program to focus on changes in behaviour, relationships, actions, and activities in the people, groups, and organizations it works with directly. In doing so, it debunks many of the myths about measuring impact. It will help a program be specific about the actors it targets, the changes it expects to see, and the strategies it employs and, as a result, be more effective in terms of the results it achieves. This publication explains the various steps in the outcome mapping approach and provides detailed information on workshop design and facilitation. It includes numerous worksheets and examples' (quoted from the synopsis of the book, available at www.idrc.ca).

- Cammack, J. (2000). *Financial Management for Development, Accounting and Finance for the Non-specialist in Development Organisations.* Oxford: INTRAC. This book has been written for non-financial staff and board members of NGOs who need to understand financial systems and statements. This work includes chapters on accounting for income-generating, financial controls and audit. Checklists are given to interpret accounts and assess financial systems. Appendices include a comprehensive glossary and information on international variations in terminology and formats.

CHAPTER 4

- Guijt, I. and J. Woodhill (2002). *A Guide for Project M&E: Managing for Impact in Rural Development.* Rome: IFAD. This book has been written for project managers and M&E staff to improve the quality of M&E in IFAD-supported projects. It helps to improve the understanding of 'progress', stimulates learning and helps to decide on actions for improved strategies and operations and to set up an M&E system. It can be downloaded from www.ifad.org and is also available in Arabic, French and Spanish.

- Davies, R. and J. Dart (2005). 'The Most Significant Change Technique: A Guide to its Use'. Available at www.mande.co.uk. Now embraced as an alternative to a rigid use of indicators, the significant change technique can help to monitor and evaluate social change and is applicable to a diversity of sectors and cultural contexts. This source provides the background theory and is useful to experienced PME practitioners and beginners alike.

- United Nations Development Programme (UNDP)/Global Environment Facility (GEF) (2005). 'Measuring and Demonstrating Impact'. This is an extensive resource kit prepared by the GEF M&E unit for guidance to all aspects of project M&E. It is available at www.undp.org.

- UNDP (2002). *Handbook on Monitoring and Evaluating for Results.* New York: UNDP Evaluation Office. This work links M&E with results-based management and is project-oriented. It is available at www.undp.org.

- Kabeer, N. (1999). *Reversed Realities. Gender Hierarchies in Development Theory.* London: Verso. This book provides the underpinning for the social relations framework or approach.

- McMilian, E. (2003). *Not-for-Profit Budgeting and Financial Management.* New Delhi: Financial Management Services Foundation. This book offers an easy-to-implement and easy-to-monitor budgeting system, written in a non-technical, 'how-to' language and format. It includes examples of relevant forms and documents and is especially useful to understand what budgeting can do management-wise, rather than being read to implement as a system.

- Gross, M., J. McCarthy and N. Shelmon (2005). *Financial and Accounting Guide for Not-for-Profit Organisations.* New York: Wiley. Now in its seventh edition, this book gives authoritative advice on financial reporting, accounting and control situations unique to voluntary organisations. It discusses key financial concepts, the presentation of financial statements, the importance of budgeting, avoiding bankruptcy, obtaining the right accountant and effective internal accounting control for voluntary organisations.

- Selener, D. (1996). *Documenting, Evaluating and Learning from Development Projects.* Quito: International Institute of Rural Reconstruction. This book is a step-by-step guide to participatory PME, with a focus on 'systematising', and provides a continuous reflection-action on both project results and processes.

- Fuerstein, M-T. (1986). *Partners in Evaluation: Evaluating Development and Community Programmes with Participants.* London: Macmillan. A pioneering basic text for participatory M&E in the form of a simple and practical handbook, with plenty of participatory research and analysis tools suitable for community work.

- Estrella, M. (2000). *Learning from Change: Issues in Participatory Monitoring and Evaluation.* London: IT Publications. This work is a collection of case studies and essays exploring conceptual, methodological and policy issues in participatory M&E from across the South.

Chapter 5

- Britton, B. (2005). *Organisational Learning in NGOs: Creating the Motives, Means and Opportunities.* Oxford: INTRAC. This work is also available at www.intrac.org. It 'Examines why NGOs need to provide the motive, means and opportunity for organisational learning, and introduces practical examples of how pioneering NGOs are doing this'. It recognises the need 'to explore innovative approaches which are relevant, appropriate and accessible across a wide range of cultures and contexts' (quoted in the website www. intrac.org).

- Kelleher, D., K. McLaren and R. Bisson (1996). *Grabbing the Tiger by the Tail: NGOs Learning for Organisational Change.* Canadian Council for International Co-operation. This is a good 'how-to' text on helping NGOs think strategically and manage change. This volume includes case studies to enhance organisational learning processes and tools to facilitate organisational growth.

- Senge, P. (1990). *The Fifth Discipline: The Art and Practice of the Learning Organisation.* New York: Doubleday/Currency. This book presents an approach to thinking and acting that can help to reduce 'learning disabilities' in organisations. It highlights the personal and team dimensions of learning, the force of mental models and the importance of a shared vision. It is based on the corporate sector, but is relevant to voluntary organisations too.

- Senge, P., A. Kleiner, C. Roberts, R.B. Ross and B.J. Smith (1995). *The Fifth Discipline Fieldbook: Strategies and Tools for Building a Learning Organisation.* London: Breadley. A companion piece to *The Fifth Discipline: The Art and Practice of the Learning Organisation* (Senge, 1990), it is more practical in its orientation, with exercises and stories to undo 'learning disabilities' and promote continuous, collective learning in the organisation. While written primarily for business entities, it has many useful exercises applicable to the voluntary sector as well.

- Pretty, J., I. Guijt, J. Thompson and I. Scoones (1995). *Participatory Learning and Action: A Trainer's Guide.* London: IIED. This is a comprehensive training guide in the use of PRA or PLA (participatory learning and action), including its theoretical background, and field and workshop methods and exercises.

CHAPTER 6

- European Union (1993). 'Manual of Project Cycle Management, Integrated Approach and Logical Framework'. *Evaluation Unit, Methods and Instruments for Project Cycle Management,* No. 1, February 1993. This paper presents a useful set of procedures to assess external factors. It can help organisations decide on their degree of importance and whether these need monitoring, how and how frequently.

- Wallace, T. with L. Bornstein and J. Chapman (2006). *The Aid Chain, Coercion and Commitment in Development NGOs.* Rugby: IT Publications. This book explores the role of funding conditions in shaping cooperation and resistance as aid moves from donors to NGOs to local communities. Findings from fieldwork in Uganda, South Africa and the UK are used to show how the fast-changing aid sector has encouraged the mainstreaming of a managerial approach at the expense of analyses of power relations or cultural diversity.

- Estrella, M. and J. Gaventa (1998). 'Who Counts Reality? Participatory M&E. A Literature Review'. IDS Working Paper No. 70, Brighton. This paper presents key principles of participatory M&E, tools and methods used, using experiences of a wide range of stakeholders across the world.

- Lewis, D. and T. Wallace (2000). *New Roles and Relevance: Development NGOs and the Challenge of Change.* Bloomfield, USA: Kumarian. This book presents a rich collection of articles analysing the changing context within which NGOs operate and its implications for impact. A number of these articles are relevant to other chapters in this volume, such as organisational learning for NGOs, perspectives on development and change, and NGOs and peace-building.

- March, C., I. Smyth and M. Mukhopadhyay (1999). *A Guide to Gender-analysis Frameworks.* Oxford: Oxfam. This book reviews a number of frameworks to analyse gender relations. It provides detailed instructions and guidance on the selection of a particular framework and has illustrative case studies.

- Fogla, M. (2001). *Legal and Finance Handbook for Voluntary Organisations—A Layman's Guide to Various Legal and Finance Legislations.* New Delhi: Financial Management Services Foundation. This work provides a near-framework for legal and accounting aspects of voluntary organisations. It is written from a layman's point of view, in a simple manner. While it is primarily useful to implementing NGOs, grant-making agencies, consultants and auditors working with NGOs in India, it contains sufficient general material to be helpful to NGOs outside India as well.

- UNDP, http://mdgmonitor.org, provides a full presentation of the millennium development goals, targets and indicators.

CHAPTER 7

- Ramashia, R. and S. Rankin (1995). *Managing Evaluation: A Guide for NGO Leadership.* Braamfontein: PACT. While written for NGO leaders themselves, this booklet looks at resistance to evaluation, ethics in evaluation and using external facilitators. It also proposes easy steps to manage an evaluation process.

- Billis, D. and M. Harris (1996). *Voluntary Agencies: Challenges of Organisation and Management.* London: MacMillan. This book explores, among others, the value bases of the voluntary sector, accountability issues, types of organisations and leadership challenges. Although its focus is on the UK, the debates are relevant to other contexts.

- Goold, L., W. Ogara and R. James (1998). 'Churches and Organisation Development in Africa: Directions and Dilemmas for Northern NGOs', INTRAC, Occasional Paper No. 20, Oxford. This paper provides a comprehensive description of the challenges faced by faith-based organisations and the capacity-building challenges that go with them.

- Edwards, E. and D. Hulme (eds) (1994). *Making a Difference: NGOs and Development in a Changing World.* London: Earthscan. This is a rich collection of essays, with one set, among others, exploring relationships between NGOs and governments and another examining the challenges of organisational growth.

- Gubbels, P. and C. Koss (2000). *From the Roots Up–Strengthening Organisational Capacity through Guided Self-assessment.* Oklahoma, USA: World Neighbours. This is an easy-to-read text to facilitate organisational growth, especially for smaller groups. It contains a number of exercises and tools and adopts a dynamic, self-help 'organisational growth' perspective.

CHAPTER 8

- Bakewell, O. (2003). 'Sharpening the Development Process. A Practical Guide to Monitoring and Evaluation'. INTRAC, Praxis Guide No. 1, Oxford. This text provides a good overview of basic M&E aspects, including information management. A separate section is dedicated to the challenges of M&E in advocacy, capacity-building and humanitarian emergencies.

- *Sphere Handbook* (2005). Oxford: Oxfam. This text aims at improving the effectiveness and accountability of disaster response, setting minimum standards for disaster assessment, participation of affected groups, gender, targeting and M&E. It is applicable to different areas of intervention in emergencies such as health, food security and water and sanitation. The book also includes training material for disaster response, including M&E. See www.sphereproject.org.

- *Drought Cycle Management. A Toolkit for the Drylands of the Greater Horn* (2004). IIRR, Acacia, CORDAID. This presents a model now adopted by governments throughout the East African region to manage droughts. It emphasises contingency planning for disaster preparedness and M&E (including in emergency stages) with strong population involvement, integrating local early warning systems.

- James, R. (2001). 'Practical Guidelines for the Monitoring and Evaluation of Capacity Building Experiences from Africa'.

INTRAC, Occasional Paper No. 36, Oxford. This paper uses a simple framework, the 'ripple model' to illustrate different result levels in capacity-building interventions. It supports the need for M&E of capacity-building, in spite of its complex nature, and provides practical tools to do so.

- Jolly, R. (ed.) (1997). *Working in Long-term Conflict: Managing the Organisational Challenge.* Oxford: INTRAC. This book sets out the main challenges, including those related to M&E, when working in conflict situations (including tools for understanding conflict, programming in conflict and organisational adaptation to conflict situations).

WEBSITES

- www.mande.co.uk. Monitoring and Evaluation News, edited by R. Davies. This site provides information about innovations in M&E methods relevant to development projects and programmes, with sections on work in progress (planned or being developed), M&E events, training cycles and conferences, publications, contact names and e-mail addresses for further information. The site includes many links with other M&E sites, M&E societies and networks.

- www.eldis.org/participation/pme/index.htm. This website is run by the Institute of Development Studies in the UK. See 'ELDIS Participation Resource Guide: Participatory Monitoring and Evaluation' and reviews of latest documents in the database.

- http://portals.wi.wur.nl/ppme. Run from Wageningen University in the Netherlands, this website has a focus on participatory PME and 'Managing and learning for impact in rural development'. It provides presentation of theories and background, methodologies and approaches, tools and methods, resources, news and events.

ABOUT THE AUTHORS

This volume has been put together by five facilitators with many years' experience of supporting PME practice in civil society organisations on all continents. John De Coninck (john@ crossculturalfoundation.or.ug) is a development consultant based in Uganda; Khilesh Chaturvedi (khilesh@askindia.org) is deputy director at ASK in New Delhi; Ben Haagsma (Ben.Haagsma@icco. nl), a rural development advisor at IC Consult in the Netherlands, supports ICCO and CORDAID development partners throughout the world. His colleague, Hans Griffioen (hpbg@bart.nl), has until recently worked as a consultant, linking financial management to organisational development issues. Mariecke van der Glas (icconica@cam.org.ni) is a researcher and presently programme coordinator for ICCO in Nicaragua. The work of these core authors has been complemented by contributions from 15 other trainers and facilitators working in consultancy organisations and NGOs in Africa, Asia and Latin America.